Mos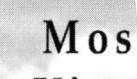
Bhante Vimalaramsi Mahāthera

*The Breath of Love*

A simple guide for Mindfulness of Breathing Meditation
with support information for Loving-kindness Meditation,
Forgiveness Meditation, and Walking Meditation

# The Breath of Love

Author
**Most Venerable Bhante Vimalaraṁsi Mahāthera**

Layout and Design
**Vidi Dayāsati**

Publisher
**Ehipassiko Foundation**

Copyright ©2012 Bhante Vimalaraṁsi
ISBN 978-602-8194-49-5
1st print: Feb 2012

**Dhamma Sukha Meditation Center**
8218 County Road 204, Annapolis, MO 63620 USA
www.dhammasukha.org
Phone: 573-5461214

# Table of Contents

# Foreword

The Buddha's Teachings are very suitable for any individual who is seeking peace and happiness, irrespective of any religious background. With this universal tradition you can practice sweet Loving-kindness ("*Mettā*" in Pāli) Meditation and become a true blessing to the whole world.

Loving-kindness is the first of four sublime states of mind. The other sublime states of mind are: compassion, appreciative joy, and equanimity. Practicing these four sublime states of mind have limitless applications and boundaries in our every-day lives. For example, Loving-kindness can be radiated towards yourself, towards family members, friends and co-workers. It can even be radiated toward all living beings under the sun and beyond. Whenever you wish someone Loving-kindness you can bring them healing, peace, and happiness.

Loving-kindness equally offers its sweet blessings on the pleasant and the unpleasant, on the rich and the poor, on the vicious and the virtuous, on females and males, as well as on human beings and non-human beings. This meditation instruction is simple to follow. It can be practiced by everyone who has the strong desire to experience more calm and joy than ever before. We all try in many different ways to pursue happiness. This is an unmistakable way to the true happiness that goes far beyond worldly materialistic types of happiness.

Some years ago in Malaysia I met the Ven. Vimalaraṁsi and was so impressed by his style of teaching meditation that I invited this always smiling monk to come and teach meditation at the Washington Buddhist Vihāra. He is not just another ordinary meditation teacher who follows the popular and modified meditation teachings of some Buddhist commentaries. This extraordinary teacher always refers to and uses the suttas as taught by the Lord Buddha in the original Pāli Canon.

I see him as a serious follower of the "Kālāma Sutta". This sutta suggests that we not follow anything without true investigation. He is continually checking and practicing to see if the teachings are in agreement with the spirit and the teachings of the suttas given by the Buddha.


**Ven. M. Dhammasiri**
President of the Washington Buddhist Vihāra

# Introduction

The most rewarding day of my life was the day I knew for certain that the Buddha-Dhamma was REAL! This Dhamma changed my life completely. It could change yours, too. Each day is a day of thanks for the Buddha, the Dhamma and the Saṅgha and for the privilege of being born within this Buddha Dispensation. What a wonderful opportunity and adventure!

The first edition of the little book "The Ānāpānasati Sutta: A Practical guide for Breathing and Tranquil Wisdom Meditation" was printed in 1995. Today the original text continues to spread worldwide. Hundreds of thousands of copies have been issued presently in 9 languages. It's even been used in universities abroad as the guide for learning meditation. Most amazing is that the book has spread on its own!

The author, Most Venerable Bhante Vimalaraṁsi Mahāthera, is a thirty plus year meditator who spent over twenty years following the commentarial explanations on how to meditate before looking in the suttas. Then he practiced according to the suttas and having seen for himself the results do not match the commentarial descriptions, Bhante put aside the commentary as he was advised to do by an elder monk. From that point on, he followed the Buddha's instructions as closely as possible.

For over sixteen years, he has dedicated himself to further investigations. He has been teaching anyone who would dare to ask the following questions directly: Did the Buddha actually find a way out of suffering in this life that was different from other meditation traditions of his time? If he did, how did he do it? Did he leave us precise instructions? Can it be done again in this day and time? Can this practice be taken into our daily lives? If so, what difference can it make?

Remember: Meditation is life! Life is meditation!

Following his enlightenment and full awakening, Buddha Gotama taught the Dhamma for a remarkable 45 years! This book is about the instructions he taught that have survived in the suttas, the discourses in the Pāli canon that were taught by the Buddha to his followers. It examines "The Ānāpānasati Sutta" from the Majjhima Nikāya: the Middle Length Sayings.

This sutta teaches us Mindfulness of Breathing through Tranquil Wisdom Insight Meditation (TWIM). The instructions are repeated several times throughout the Pāli Canon using the same identical words. This repetition confirms the importance of these instructions. Sometimes phrases in a sutta indicate the instructions over again.

It is said that there are more than forty objects of meditation that the Buddha taught. However, all these forms dealt with one goal in particular, that is, reaching a clear understanding of the impersonal process of Dependent Origination and the Four Noble Truths. This book is about using the breath as the object of the meditation to do just that.

The result of this practice is seeing for oneself the true nature of things. Students who have put forth a sincere effort to follow these instructions precisely have made remarkable strides in their meditation progress.

Bhante Vimalaraṁsi brings these teachings to life using simple clear wording. To study with Bhante Vimalaraṁsi is a refreshing rediscovery of our inherent altruistic joy and an introduction to what, according to the Buddha, a guiding teacher should actually be. The Buddha indicates that a guiding teacher should be a sincere conduit of the Buddha's words, emboldening his students to listen carefully, investigate fully, observe accurately, frequently question and confirm everything through personal experience.

Here's the amazing thing. What the Buddha did is not mythical, strictly religious, or philosophical. It's real! I've been investigating it for over eleven years now. It is a methodical scientific experiment which uncovers how mind's attention moves and leads to the discovery of the true nature of HOW everything works in life. It piques one's curiosity and alters our perspective. It becomes all too clear why this particular practice changed the world in the Buddha's time.

Buddhist meditation is the compassionate groundbreaking discovery leading to a doorway that reveals a pathway for transcendence to peace. To make peace a reality, mankind only needs to activate this practice. The doorway is available just as it was in the time of the Buddha! We have to choose to go through it.

Bhante has been bold in his approach to the practice and continues to reach into the heart of the Buddha's teaching with his own questions as he trains his students. He knows this is a journey you must personally take for yourself to reach a full understanding of this Dhamma. He sets the Dhamma Wheel in motion as you begin your journey and challenges you to make the effort to reach the destination for yourself.

If you work with Bhante as your guiding teacher, you will discover the true nature of suffering, how it is caused, and how to find great relief in this life. He offers you the next step each time you interview with him. Your progress is directly proportional to how well you follow the instructions, your accurate investigation through meditation, and your willingness to ask questions.

After 2600 years, the Buddha-Dhamma has become a bit diluted. This is to be expected with any teaching this old. It is important that we consider a slight realignment to get across to people today that "Meditation is Life and Life is Meditation".

If we follow the Buddha's last wishes and go to the suttas instead of recreating the teachings on our own, we will find that there are the same 37 requisites for awakening that, when clearly understood and fully experienced, can set us free. These requisites are like the threads set upon a loom, ready to be woven into a balanced cloth.

If these teachings are taught as separate spools of yarn sitting in a basket, the student may never realize that, when set upon the loom and woven together, a bright tapestry can be woven with a pattern of perfect symmetry and beauty that is the Dhamma Cloth! When these "spools of yarn" are studied apart from the loom, we have great difficulty realizing any finished product or understanding how this can help us today. But set upon the loom, in balance together, these spools of yarn give us the answers we seek: the true nature of how things actually are and how we can become happier living with this.

This practice is like a fine recipe. Don't leave out ANY ingredients! Don't change the instructions! Just do it. Find out for yourself the relief promised by the Buddha. Come and see!

Let this book be a guide to your deeper understanding of the Dhamma. Use it well and often. Pass it along to others.

**Rev. Sister Khema**
United International Buddha-Dhamma Society, Inc.
Dhamma Sukha Meditation Center
and Anathapindika's Study Park

# 1
# The Ānāpānasati Sutta

## A Practical Guide to
## Mindfulness of Breathing and
## Tranquil Wisdom Meditation

### Please Note

Some additional materials appear in this version of this book. As usual, the Ānāpānasati Sutta explains in full the sutta with regard to your meditation instructions. All parts of the Ānāpānasati Sutta are printed in **bold upright letters**. All other supporting sutta references used are printed in ***bold italics***. In this edition, three other primary practices are explained. They are Loving-kindness Meditation, Forgiveness Meditation and the specific instructions for Walking Meditation which should accompany all practices. A glossary of terms is added in the order you would study the meditation. We hope this will be good support for your TWIM practice.

# An Open Invitation

Many people are now on a search for a spiritual path that leads their mind to peace and happiness. They discovered that the norms of the world which emphasize material happiness, do not actually bring real peace and security.

Instead, those norms lead to more pain and dissatisfaction. For these people, the Buddha's Noble Eightfold Path exemplifies a simple and contented life; a life that is open and free. The Buddha taught the method to free our minds of lust, hatred and delusion. He started by showing his disciples how to have an open mind that expands beyond its present limitations so that you can examine with understanding how everything works.

In the Kālāma Sutta, the Buddha explicitly stated that you should not follow any beliefs blindly, but rather, you should always examine and investigate for yourself. These admonishments were put forth for the purpose of opening and expanding your experience so that you will not be attached to any particular doctrine without thorough investigation.

This kind of honest inquiry into any particular doctrine opens on your mind and expands your consciousness. Then, you will see what leads to a close or tight mind and what leads to a mind that is open and clear.

One of the many lessons the Buddha teaches is to first, expand your consciousness by the practice of generosity (*dāna*). When a person is miserly, they have a tendency to have a tight and limited mind full of craving. Their mind holds onto material things and easily becomes attached to them. Attachment of any form makes mind uncomfortable and tense.

This tension is the cause of immeasurable pain and suffering (*dukkha*). Thus, by encouraging the practice of generosity, it teaches us how to have a joyful, open, and clear mind which is never closed or tight.

Another form of generosity is the giving of time and energy to help those who are having problems, i.e. to become real friends. This includes helping others to be happy! When we say or perform actions which cause people to smile, it opens our mind and then joy arises. This doesn't only happen to the other person but in our own mind as well. This type of practice helps us to expand our mind and let go of the tension.

**Precepts**

The Buddha also emphasizes the importance of keeping our moral discipline (*sīla*). The precepts are not commandments but rather they are suggestions to follow. Keeping them leads to a mind that easily becomes calm and composed. These five moral precepts release mind from remorse, anxiety, and guilty feelings if they are continually kept and observed.

These precepts are:
1. Abstaining from killing or harming living beings on purpose;
2. Abstaining from taking what is not given;
3. Abstaining from wrong sexual activities;
4. Abstaining from telling lies, using harsh language, slandering, and gossip;
5. Abstaining from taking drugs and alcohol that dull our

mind (this does not mean a doctor's prescriptions; just drugs or alcohol for the purpose of taking the edge off of daily living).

Keeping these precepts closely means that our mind will be tension and guilt-free.

Subsequently, the Buddha taught the methods of meditation or mental development (bhāvanā), to free mind from tension and confusion. The essence of meditation is to open and calm your mind and accept whatever arises without any tightening at all.

This book of instructions is written for those who are on this noble quest. To a beginner, these instructions may appear confusing and difficult to understand. However, you will gradually discover the many benefits when these instructions are followed closely.

In actual fact, within the texts, meditation, as taught by the Buddha, is never broken into different kinds of meditation. It is never taken to be deep concentration in any of its forms, that is, fixed or absorption concentration (appanā samādhi), access or neighborhood concentration (upacāra samādhi) or moment-to-moment concentration (khanika samādhi), which actually brings tightness to mind and suppresses the hindrances.

The 'concentration' meditation is a form of suppression, a kind of cutting off of your experience which causes a kind of resistance to arise in your mind. As a result, there is a conflict with reality.

On the other hand, "Tranquil Wisdom Insight Meditation" (TWIM), as found within the texts, opens mind and is continually expanding it. It does not ever exclude or resist anything. A 'concentrated' mind does not meditate in the "Buddha's Way".

It doesn't matter whether you are talking about full or fixed absorption concentration, or access concentration. These still cause the same difficulties in practice.

The important rule of the meditation is, no matter what distracts your mind away from the breath and tranquilizing your mind, you simply open, expand, let it go without thinking about the distraction, relax mind and tightness in the head. As you feel mind open and relax away the tension, you lightly smile, and softly redirect your attention back to the object of meditation i.e. the breath and relaxing on the in-breath and relaxing on the out-breath.

Next is the Pāli word *samatha*. The more accurate meanings of *samatha* are peacefulness, calmness, tranquility, serenity or stillness and not as the commonly translated terms of absorption or fixed concentration. Thus, the author prefers to use the word tranquility.

The Pāli word *samādhi* is equally important as it has many different meanings such as calmness, unified mind, tranquility, peacefulness, stillness, composure of mind, quiet mind, serenity, and one of the lesser meanings, "concentration". Thus, the true meaning is not merely fixed absorption concentration or access concentration, but calmness or stillness in different degrees. Interestingly, Rhys Davids found through his studies, that the word '*samādhi*' was never used before the time of the Buddha. [2]

Even though, as a Bodhisatta, he practiced 'absorption meditation', the word *samādhi* has a different meaning other than concentration. The Buddha "popularized" the word *samādhi* to express collectedness, calm wisdom, tranquility, openness, awareness, along with developing a mind which has clarity and wisdom in it. Later, the Hindus changed the meaning to 'concentration'. Hence, the author will use collectedness, stillness, composure of mind, or unified mind for the meaning here.

If one chooses to use the word **'concentration'**, they must understand that it means 'collectedness of mind', 'composure of mind', or 'a unified mind'. It does not mean absorption, fixed (*appanā*), or access (*upacāra*) concentration or even momentary (*khanika*) concentration.

This book is written with a deep conviction that serenity and insight were yoked together in the Buddha's practice. It is committed to the understanding that the systematic cultivation of 'Tranquil Wisdom Insight Meditation' (TWIM) brings both serenity of mind AND the insights needed to realize the true nature of this psycho/physical (mind/body) process together at the same time!

Furthermore, there is the seeing and realizing the cause and effect relationships of all dependent conditions. This means seeing the impersonal process of Dependent Origination and the Four Noble Truths, which, in fact, is the development of penetrative wisdom that leads to dispassion, emancipation and awakening. As a matter of fact, the Buddha discovered that 'concentration practices' of any kind did not lead him to *Nibbāna*.

After becoming a homeless one, the Bodhisatta went to two different teachers of "absorption concentration meditation". His first teacher was Āḷāra Kālāma. After learning the Dhamma and discipline, he practiced until he attained a very high and distinguished stage of meditation called the "realm of nothingness". The Bodhisatta then went to his teacher and asked whether he could proceed any further with that meditation.

Āḷāra Kālāma replied that it was the highest stage that anyone could attain.

The Bodhisatta was dissatisfied and went to another teacher by the name of Uddaka Rāmaputta.      He learned that Dhamma and discipline and then practiced it and attained the "realm of neither perception nor non-perception". The Bodhisatta again went to his teacher and asked a similar question about there being more to attain. Again, the Bodhisatta was told that this was absolutely the highest attainment anyone could achieve in their lifetime.

The future Buddha was disappointed because he saw that there were still many more things to let go of in his mind. He observed that these "absorption concentration techniques", which focused intensely on the object of meditation, caused **tightening** in mind.

The Buddha reasoned that there was still attachment whenever there was tension in mind. He also noticed that if any part of the experiences were suppressed or not allowed to arise, there was still some kind of holding on or attachment to an ego belief. This occurs with every form of 'concentration', that is, fixed absorption concentration, or access concentration,

Thus, after six long years of trying all of the various spiritual and ascetic practices from body mortifications like starving the body, to holding the breath, he realized that these practices did not lead him to a calm and open mind which was free from craving and suffering.

On the night of the Bodhisatta's realization of supreme *Nibbāna*, he recalled an incident at a plowing festival while he was just a young boy of one or two years old. When his attendants left him alone under a rose-apple tree, he sat in "Tranquil Wisdom Insight Meditation" (TWIM) and experienced a mind that was expanded and opened! He saw that this form of meditation would lead him to the experience of "tranquility *Jhānas*", as opposed to 'concentration *Jhānas*'.[3]

As a result of the gentle "Tranquil Wisdom Insight Meditation" (TWIM), his mind was filled with joy, his body became light and happy. When the joy faded away, he then experienced strong calmness and peacefulness. His mind and body became very comfortable. His mind was very still, very composed, and his body was exceptionally at ease, with sharp mindfulness and full awareness of what was happening around him . He could still hear sounds and feel sensations with his body at that time.

When the Bodhisatta sat under the Bodhi tree to meditate on the full moon night of May and made his great effort to attain supreme *Nibbāna*, he recalled that not all forms of pleasure are unwholesome. He realized that there could be pleasurable feelings arising in mind and body although there was not an attachment to anything. [refer to MN-36]

That very night, the Bodhisatta practiced "Tranquil Wisdom Insight Meditation" (TWIM) through the method of opening, relaxing, and expanding mind. In short, he practiced the "Ānāpānasati" or "Mindfulness of Breathing" and the 6R's which are the steps of Right Effort. As we all know, he became the Buddha or the Supremely Awakened One.

The Ānāpānasati Sutta, as taught by the Buddha 2600 years ago, still provides the most simple, direct, thorough, and effective method for training and developing the 6R's and smiling through our daily tasks and any problems as well as for our highest aim—mind's own unshakable deliverance from greed, hatred and delusion, which, is another way of saying craving).

The simple steps that are the 6R's and the practice of smiling into our daily tasks are what this sutta is really communicating to us. The method described here is taken directly from the sutta itself and the results can be seen clearly and easily when you practice according to the instructions in this sutta.

The author would like to emphasize that the instructions in this book are not his "own opinion". Actually, these are the Buddha's own instructions given in a clear and precise way. This can be called the "Undiluted Dhamma" because it comes directly from the suttas themselves, without a lot of additions or free-lance ideas.

The Ānāpānasati Sutta gives the most profound meditation instructions available today. It includes the "Four Foundations of Mindfulness" and the "Seven Awakening Factors" and shows how they are fulfilled through the practice of "Mindfulness of Breathing". This is done through attaining all of the meditation stages of understanding (*Jhānas*).[4] This sutta shows the direct way to practice "Tranquil Wisdom Insight Meditation" (TWIM) and does not mix in any other meditation practices.

Strangely, the current separation into various types of meditation like "fixed absorption concentration", or "access concentration" and "momentary concentration" seems to appear only in the commentaries and never in the suttas. Thus, you must notice this and compare these commentaries with the suttas for their accuracy.

Upon the attainment of the fourth *Jhāna*, three alternative lines of further development become possible. This sutta deals with only one of those lines, namely the attainment of all the material and immaterial *Jhānas* (meditation stages of understanding), followed by the experience of the cessation of perception, feeling. and consciousness (nirodha samapatti in Pāli), and finally the experience of seeing clearly the links of Dependent Origination (*Paṭicca-Samuppāda*) and the Four Noble Truths (*Ariyasacca*).

In these attainments, the Buddha mentions four meditative stages that continue the mental unification established by the *Jhānas*, meditation stages of understanding. These states are described as "the liberations that are peaceful and material", (*rūpa*), and they are still mundane states.

These mundane states are distinguished from the immaterial (*arūpa*) *Jhānas*, meditation stages of understanding, which then deepen the subtle mental observations, and are named after their own exalted stages: "the base of infinite space, the base of infinite consciousness, the base of nothingness, and the base of neither perception nor non-perception."

These states of consciousness are very attainable if one ardently and continually keeps their daily meditation practice going. As this is a gradual training, you first must learn to walk before you run. Thus, the beginning of the meditation practice is the basis for further development.

This is a straight and direct path towards liberation and the supramundane *Nibbāna*. It does, however, require sustained meditative effort, applied to a simple object of meditation to the breath and relaxing. This allows the mind to become calm and clear without distractions.

When you practice the Ānāpānasati Sutta as a "Tranquil Wisdom Insight Meditation" (TWIM), you will find that your creativity and intuition increase as your practice develops.

This approach forms the timeless and universal appeal of a true 'Doctrine of Awakening', that is, realizing Dependent Origination and the Four Noble Truths, which has the depth and breadth, the simplicity and intelligence for providing the foundation of a living Dhamma for all. You will sense the urgency of the fundamental "non-materialistic" problems and search for solutions that neither science nor "religions of faith" provide.

More important is the final realization which comes through the method of "Tranquil Wisdom Insight Meditation" (TWIM). This practice invites you to experience the various meditation stages of understanding (*Jhānas*) and allows you to see through direct knowledge, all twelve impersonal links of "Dependent Arising".

This means you will see and realize directly the first, second, third and fourth Noble Truths in each of the links. When these Four Noble Truths have been seen and realized directly, you will truly understand the Buddha's Teachings. This is because one cannot see the "Origin of Suffering" without first seeing the "Suffering" itself and suffering would not cease without practicing the way leading to the cessation of suffering (the 8-Fold Path which includes the 6R's). Thus, seeing and realizing Dependent Origination, means that you see and realize all of the Four Noble Truths, which is actually the true essence of Buddhist meditation.

The true aim of the Ānāpānasati Sutta is nothing less than final liberation from suffering which is the highest goal of the Buddha's Teachings—*Nibbāna*. The practice of the Buddhist Path evolves in two distinct stages, a mundane (*lokiya*) or preparatory stage, and a supramundane (*lokuttara*) or accomplished stage.

The mundane path is developed when the disciples undertake the gradual training to develop their virtues (continually keeping the precepts), collectedness, or deep composure of mind, and wisdom. This reaches its peak in the practice of "Tranquil Wisdom Insight Meditation" (TWIM), which deepens direct experience, and at the same time, shows you the Three Characteristics of all Existence that are: impermanence (*anicca*), suffering (*dukkha*) and the impersonal nature of existence (*anattā*).

In short, there are two kinds of *Nibbāna*. One is the worldly or mundane type of *Nibbāna* and the other is the supramundane or unworldly type of *Nibbāna*. The mundane or worldly type of *Nibbāna* is attained every time the meditator lets go of craving and relief arises along with a kind of happiness. This type of *Nibbāna* will occur many times when one is seriously practicing "Tranquil Wisdom Insight Meditation" (TWIM). The supramundane type of *Nibbāna* only occurs after the meditator sees and realizes 'Dependent Origination' (*Paticca-Samuppāda*) and the four Noble Truths. This supramundane *Nibbāna* takes patience and effort to achieve.

It is not impossible for laymen and laywomen to attain the supermundane state of *Nibbāna*. With persistent daily practice and by taking an occasional meditation retreat with a competent guide who understands how the "Tranquil Wisdom Insight Meditation" works, even those who live active lives in the world can still achieve this highest goal.

It was mentioned in the Parinibbāna Sutta, that during the time of the Buddha, many more laymen and laywomen became saints than the monks and bhikkhunis when they practiced on a regular basis. The common belief that one must be a 'monk' or 'nun' in order to reach this goal is just not true. The exhortation of the Buddha was for all people who were interested in the correct path. He encouraged them to ... *'Ehipassiko'* (a Pāli word meaning 'come and see'). This is very good advice because it helps those who are interested to get out of their judgmental, critical mind and honestly practice to see if this is, in fact, the right way. (See sutta number 73 The Greater Discourse to Vacchagotta in the Majjhima Nikāya for confirmation of lay people attaining *Nibbāna*).

## The Buddha Taught Dependent Origination

Dependent Origination is the teaching which makes the Buddha's path unique amongst all other types of meditation. During his period of struggle for awakening, Dependent Origination came as a marvelous and eye-opening discovery that ended his pursuit in the darkness:

*"Arising, arising—thus, Monks, in regard to things unheard before there arose in me vision, knowledge, wisdom, understanding and radiance."* (Saṁyutta Nikāya XII. 65/ii.105).

*"Once Awakened, the mission of the Tathagata is to proclaim Dependent Origination (along with the Four Noble Truths.) to the world."* (Saṁyutta Nikāya XII.25-6).

The Buddha taught this in discourse after discourse, so much so, that the Dependent Origination soon becomes the most essential and important teaching of all. When the *Arahat* Assaji was asked to state the Master's message as precisely and as briefly as possible, he gave the doctrine of arising and ceasing of Dependent Origination and the arising once again of these phenomena.

With a single sentence, the Buddha dispels doubt about the correctness of this summary: *"He who sees Dependent*

*Origination sees the Dhamma, he who sees the Dhamma sees Dependent Origination."* (Taken from the Middle Length Sayings [Majjhima Nikāya], sutta number 28, section 28). This means seeing and realizing all of the Noble Truths in all of the links of Dependent Origination. This is the only way!

When your faculties have gained a degree of maturity and you see the twelve links of 'Dependent Origination' clearly, the mundane path rises to the supramundane path because it leads directly and surely out of 'Suffering'. You then realize 'The Origin of Suffering', 'The Cessation of Suffering', and 'The Path Leading to the Way Out of Suffering'.

There is another interesting sutta about the seeing of the Four Noble Truths, found in the Dīgha Nikāya sutta number 16, section 5.27. From this section of the sutta, you can conclude that the way to attain awakening is by following the Eightfold Path and realizing the links of Dependent Origination and the Four Noble Truths. It says:

5.27] *"In whatever Dhamma and Discipline the Noble Eightfold Path is not found, no ascetic is found of the first grade (meaning a Sotāpanna), second grade (meaning Sakadāgāmī), third grade (meaning Anāgāmī), or fourth grade (meaning an Arahat). But such ascetics can be found, of the first, second, third, and fourth grade in a Dhamma and Discipline where the Noble Eightfold Path is found. Now, Subhada, in this Dhamma and Discipline the Noble Eightfold Path is found, and in it are to be found ascetics of the first, second, third and fourth grade. Those other schools are devoid of [true] ascetics; but if in this one the monks were to live to perfection, the world would not lack for Arahats."*

Mind opens when it sees and realizes these twelve impersonal links of Dependent Origination directly. As a result, mind becomes dispassionate and free. This is as true now in present times, as it was 2600 years ago. Any teaching that doesn't highlight the necessity of Dependent Origination as its realization and final goal or destination isn't teaching the true path. Currently, many people say that seeing impermanence, suffering, and not-self is realizing *Nibbāna*.

However, you must note that although these characteristics do lead the way to realizing *Nibbāna* and are very important to develop, they don't directly allow you to see the supramundane state of *Nibbāna*.

*"You can see, one or all of the three characteristics of existence, i.e., impermanence, suffering and not-self, without ever directly seeing Dependent Origination, but, when you see Dependent Origination directly you will always see all of the three characteristics."*

According to the first sutta in the Mahā Vagga of the Vinaya, it cannot work any other way.

**The Courage to Investigate**

Currently, there seems to be some disputes regarding the kinds of meditation the Buddha taught. One school of thought says—"You must begin by practicing '*Jhāna* [fixed] absorption concentration meditation' and then proceed to the fourth *Jhāna* [5] before switching over to the practice of '*Vipassanā* meditation' or momentary concentration [*khanika samādhi*].

Other schools of thought say that you can attain *Nibbāna* without going through the *Jhānas*,[6] by only practicing "*Vipassanā* meditation"[7] or developing access concentration [*upacāra samādhi*] right from the beginning of your meditation practice.

Interestingly, the word *"Vipassanā'* or 'vidassana' ,which has the same meaning, is only mentioned very few times by itself in the suttas, however, the word *Jhāna* is mentioned many thousands of times in the suttas, so what do you think the Buddha taught most?

The words Serenity (*Jhāna*) and Insight (*Vipassanā*) are mentioned together many times 'together' in the texts. In Majjhima Nikāya, sutta number 149, section 10 it says that *"serenity and insight are evenly yoked together"*.

Moreover, the Ānāpānasati Sutta shows that the Buddha taught only one kind of meditation by simultaneously developing both the *Jhānas* and wisdom. Here, the word *Jhāna* means meditation stages of understanding, not deep absorption or fixed concentration (*appanā samādhi*) or access concentration (*upacāra samādhi*).

This sutta actually shows the method of how to tranquilize mind and develop wisdom at the same time by seeing the true nature of existence. This means observing *anicca* (impermanence), *dukkha* (suffering), *anattā* (not-self), along with seeing and realizing the cause and effect relationships of Dependent Origination.

At the same time, it also fulfills the "Four Foundations of Mindfulness and the Seven Awakening Factors". Hence, the way leading to the realization of Supramundane *Nibbāna* is clearly and precisely taught in this wonderful sutta.

The commentaries have divided "concentration" and *"Vipassanā"* into different forms of meditation. This kind of "separation" does NOT appear in the suttas. Although it is mentioned in the Anguttara Nikāya that the first part of the practice is *samatha* and the second part is vidassana (developing wisdom), it is not saying that they are two different types of practices or meditations. The practice combines both into one integral system!

It is only that different things are seen at different times, as in the case of Sutta 111 'One by One as They Occurred' from the Majjhima Nikāya. This sutta gives an explanation of Venerable Sāriputta's meditation development and experience of all the *Jhānas* (meditation stages of understanding) before he attained Arahatship.

When you start to differentiate and categorize meditation practices, the situation becomes very confusing. This is also evident in the popular commentaries like the Visuddhi Magga and its sub-commentaries. You can begin to see inconsistencies when you make a comparison with the suttas. Nowadays, most scholars use just a line or parts of a sutta to ensure that the commentaries agree with that sutta.

However, if you were to read that same entire sutta, that sutta referred to may turn out to have an entirely different meaning. This is not to say that scholars are intentionally making wrong statements, but sometimes they get caught looking at tiny details or parts of the Dhamma with such a narrow view that they tend to lose a truth.

The description of the fixed absorption *Jhānas* as found in the Visuddhi Magga doesn't exactly match the description given in the suttas and, in most cases, these *Jhānas* are very different from what is found in the suttas.

For example, the Visuddhi Magga talks about having a sign (*nimitta* in Pāli). This can be a light or other visualized mind-made pictures which arise in mind at certain times when you are practicing *Jhāna* meditation (absorption concentration [*appanā samādhi*] or when you get into access concentration [*upacāra samādhi*]). With each type of 'concentration' a *nimitta* of some kind arises.

When this happens, you are practicing a 'concentration' type of meditation practice like what the Bodhisatta rejected as being the way to *Nibbāna*! However, if you were to check the suttas, the description of *nimittas* arising in mind has never been mentioned. If it were very important, it would be mentioned many times. The Buddha never taught concentration techniques, having *nimittas* (signs) arising, or the chanting of mantras. These are forms of Hindu practices that have been sneaking into Buddhism for a few hundred years.

Their influences can be seen in the 'concentration practices' and in the Tibetan Buddhist styles of meditation as well as in other popular commentaries like the Visuddhi Magga.

Thus, the current ways of practicing "concentration", does not conform to the descriptions given in the suttas. You must always honestly and openly investigate what is being said by placing it beside what is found in the suttas. It is best that you do not do this with just part of a sutta but use the whole sutta. This is because taking out one or two lines from various sections can cause confusion.

When honestly questioning what the Buddha's Teachings are, you will find that an open investigation helps you to see more clearly and thus, questions will be answered more rationally. You must always remember that the commentaries are the authors' interpretation of what the suttas say and mean.

Many times well-intentioned monks look for ways to expand their understanding and attempt to help themselves and others with their comments. Then, as time goes by, more scholar monks will expound on a certain comment explaining different subtle meanings of some tiny phrases and individual comments. This "dilutes" the true teachings and thus, has the tendency to move you further away from the true meaning and understanding of the suttas. As a result, many puzzling questions arise.

For example: In the practice of momentary concentration, where does Dependent Origination fit into the scheme of things? This practice doesn't seem to go hand in hand with the teaching of Dependent Origination.

Another question is: According to the suttas, Right Effort means bringing up zeal, or joyful interest, or enthusiasm (*chanda*) in mind. However, some meditation teachers say Right Effort only means "noting" and others say it means 'work harder'.

Other puzzling questions asked: Which suttas mention the terms momentary [*khanika samādhi*], access [*upacāra samādhi*], and absorption or fixed concentration [*appanā samādhi*] states? Which sutta describes 'Insight Knowledges'?

Which sutta says that there is no mindfulness while in the *Jhāna* meditation stages of understanding?

Please note that in the Parinibbāna Sutta, the Buddha had requested his disciples to always compare any information against the suttas and Vinaya not any other texts.

## The Kālāma Sutta

There must come a time when you stop repeating the words of others, and stop practicing questionable methods without doing some open and honest investigation into the original teachings of the Buddha.

You must not depend on hearsay, or blind belief in what any teacher says, simply because he is the authority.

In the Kālāma Sutta, the Buddha gives some very wise advice:

- It is unwise to simply believe what you hear because it has been said over and over again for a long time.
- It is unwise to follow tradition blindly just because it has been practiced in that way for a long time.
- It is unwise to listen to and spread rumors and gossip.
- It is unwise to take anything as being the absolute truth just because it agrees with your scriptures (this especially means commentaries and sub-commentaries).
- It is unwise to foolishly make assumptions, without investigation.
- It is unwise to abruptly draw a conclusion by what you see and hear without further investigation.
- It is unwise to go by mere outward appearances or to hold too tightly to any view or idea simply because you are comfortable with it.
- It is unwise to be convinced of anything out of respect and deference to your spiritual teacher without honest investigation into what is being taught.

We must go beyond opinions, beliefs, and dogmatic thinking. In this way, we can rightly reject anything, which, when accepted, practiced and perfected, leads to more anger, criticism, conceit, pride, greed, and delusion. These unwholesome states of mind are universally condemned and are certainly not beneficial to ourselves or to others. They are to be avoided whenever possible.

On the other hand, we can rightly accept anything which when practiced and perfected, leads to unconditional love, contentment and gentle wisdom. These things allow us to develop a happy, tranquil, and peaceful mind. Thus, the wise praise all kinds of unconditional love (loving acceptance of the present moment), tranquility, contentment and gentle wisdom and encourage everyone to practice these good qualities as much as possible.

In the Parinibbāna Sutta, the Buddha's advice to the monks is very plain and precise. We are to practice according to the scriptural texts and observe whether the practice is done correctly. Only after close examination and practice, along with personal experience, can you be sure that the scriptures are correct. Thus, the Buddha's advice to the monks is not only to use the suttas, but also to check whether the suttas are correct according to the Dhamma and the Discipline (Vinaya).

This is how you make sure that the information is true and can then be practiced correctly. This is taken from the Dīgha Nikāya, sutta number 16, section 4.7 to 4.11. This translation come from the book "Thus Have I Heard" by Maurice Walsh. It says:

*4.7] At Bhogangagara the Lord stayed at the Ānanda Shrine. And here he said to the monks: "Monks, I will teach you four criteria. Listen, pay close attention, and I will speak.' 'Yes sir' replied the Monks.*

*4.8] "Suppose a Monk were to say: 'Friends, I heard and received this from the Lord's own lips: this is the Dhamma, this is the Discipline, this is the Master's teaching', then Monks, you should neither approve nor disapprove his words. Then, without approving or disapproving his words and expressions this should be carefully noted and compared with the Suttas and reviewed in the light of the Discipline. If they, on such comparison and review, are found not to conform to the Suttas and the Discipline, the conclusion must be:*

*"Assuredly this is not the word of the Buddha, it has been wrongly understood by this monk; and the matter is to be rejected. But if here on such comparison and review they are found to conform to the Suttas and the Discipline, the conclusion must be: "Assuredly this is the word of the Buddha, it has been rightly understood by this Monk." This is the first criterion.*

4.9] *"Suppose a Monk were to say: "In such and such a place there is a community with elders and distinguished teachers. I have heard and received this from that community"; then, monks you should neither approve nor disapprove his words. Then, without approving or disapproving, his words and expressions should be carefully noted and compared with the Suttas and reviewed in the light of the Discipline. But where on such comparison and review, they are found not to conform to the Suttas and Discipline, the conclusion must be:*

*"Assuredly this is not the word of the Buddha, it has been wrongly understood by this monk"; and the matter is to be rejected. But where on such comparison and review they are found to conform to the suttas and the Discipline, the conclusion must be: "Assuredly this is the word of the Buddha, it has been rightly understood by this monk." That is the second criterion.*

4.10] *"Suppose a monk were to say: "In such and such a place there are many elders who are learned, bearers of the tradition, who know the Dhamma, the Discipline, the code of rules: I have heard and received this from those Monks, ... this is the Dhamma, this is the Discipline, this is the Master's teaching", then, Monks, you should neither approve nor disapprove his words. Then, without approving or disapproving, his words and expressions should be carefully noted and compared with the suttas and reviewed in the light of the Discipline. But where on such comparison and review, these are found not to conform to the suttas and the Discipline, the conclusion must be:..."and the matter is to be rejected.*

*But where on such comparison and review they are found to conform to the suttas and the Discipline, the conclusion must be: "Assuredly this is the word of the Buddha; it has been rightly understood by the monk." This is the third criterion.*

**4.11]** *"Suppose a Monk were to say: "In such and such a place there is one elder who is learned ... I have heard and received this from that elder ... this is the Dhamma, this is the Discipline, this is the Master's teaching, then, Monks, you should neither approve nor disapprove his words. Then, without approving or disapproving his words and expressions, this should be carefully noted and compared with the suttas and be reviewed in the light of the Discipline. Where on such comparison and review, this is found not to conform to the suttas and the Discipline, the conclusion must be:*

*"Assuredly this is not the word of the Buddha, it has been wrongly understood by this Monk; and the matter is to be rejected.*

*But where such comparison and review they are found to conform to the suttas and the Discipline, the conclusion must be. "Assuredly this is the word of the Buddha; it has been rightly understood by the Monk." This is the fourth criterion.*

The spirit of open investigation and exploration into the ways and means of the Buddha's Middle Path is open to all who have an inquiring mind. This means a mind which is not stuck in looking at things through pride and attachment at what they "think" is right without first checking with the suttas.[8] Occasionally, some meditators become so much attached to their opinions and teachers such that they think their method is the "only way", without checking the true teachings from the suttas.

As this book is taken directly from the suttas, you can observe how things can be confused and misrepresented by some commentaries. If you have the courage to investigate and practice, you will be pleasantly surprised at the simplicity and clarity of the Buddha's teaching, especially when commentaries like the Visuddhi Magga are left alone. Although the suttas appear dry and repetitive, they are quite illuminating and can be fun to read, especially when you practice the meditation and gain intellectual knowledge at the same time.

**Prelude to Tranquil Wisdom Insight Meditation (TWIM)**

Before you start practicing the meditation, it is very important to build a strong foundation of morality (sīla). If you don't even practice the five precepts, you will lose interest and finally stop meditating, because you think that the technique is incorrect.

Actually the Buddha's technique works very well. This is just a case of not having the complete practice and not doing it in the correct way. Keeping the precepts is essential to the development and purity of mind. If you break any of these precepts, you will experience a lot of restlessness, remorse, and anxiety due to your guilty feelings. This causes mind to be tight and clouds your thoughts.

These precepts are absolutely necessary for any spiritual attainments. They support your general mindfulness and awareness to help you to have a peaceful mind that is clear from any remorse due to wrong doing. A peaceful calm mind is a mind that is tension-free and clear.

Thus, it is a very good idea to take these precepts every day, not as some form of rite or ritual, but as a reminder for your practice. Taking the precepts every day helps to keep your mind, speech, and actions uplifted. There are people who recite these precepts in the Pāli language. However, it can turn into an empty exercise if you don't completely understand Pāli. For the earnest meditator it is best to recite these precepts daily in a language that you understand so that the meanings are clear without a doubt.

These precepts are:

**1.] I undertake to keep the precept to abstain from killing or harming living beings on purpose.**

This precept includes non-killing of beings like ants, mosquitoes, wasps or cockroaches, etc.

**2.] I undertake to keep the precept to abstain from taking what is not given.**

This covers any forms of stealing which even includes taking a pencil from work without permission or using equipment like copy machines for personal use.

**3.] I undertake to keep the precept to abstain from wrong sexual activity.**

Basically, it means not having any sexual activity with another person's partner, or having sexual activity with someone that is still under the care of a family member. It also means that one must follow the sexual laws of the land.

Any sexual activity that causes undue pain to another being will cause one to have remorse and guilty feelings to arise.

**4.] I undertake to keep the precept to abstain from telling lies, using harsh speech, slandering others, and speaking gossip or nonsense talk.**

This means abstinence from any type of speech which is not true or helpful to others. It also includes abstinence from telling white lies.

**5.] I undertake to keep the precept to abstain from taking drugs and alcohol which dulls mind.**

Many people think that drinking one glass of beer or one social glass of wine or smoking a joint of marijuana would not affect their mind. But this is not true! If you are seriously practicing meditation, you become very sensitive and will notice the effects of even taking something as harmless as aspirin. It can dull your mind for a whole day. How much more will this happen with alcohol and other drugs?

However, when you are sick and the doctor says that you must take a certain drug as medicine, then please take the medicine. This precept refers to taking drugs or alcohol in order to relax and escape from the stress of the day.

As soon as you realize that you have broken a precept, you should first forgive yourself and acknowledge that you are not perfect. This helps you to free your mind a little. You then retake the precepts as soon as possible and make a determination not to break the precepts again.

Taking the precepts again will help to re-purify mind. Over a period of time, you will become more aware and naturally abstain from breaking them because you realize these harmful effects.

Please practice only one meditation technique at a time because mind will become confused if you try to mix and match various meditations. Mixing and matching only stops your progress.

How do you find a good teacher? The best way is to pick only one teacher who truly understands the meditation and can explain things clearly and precisely.

The way to select a good teacher is by seeing if the teacher is teaching you about how to know and recognize the links of Dependent Origination and the Four Noble Truths. Then, stay with that teacher for a period of time and see for yourself whether your mind becomes more happy and peaceful; not just while meditating, but in daily life as well. This is ultimately the best way to choose.

Does your awareness of mind states become clearer and easier to recognize, can you let go of them, relax and smile during your daily activities as well as during the sitting practice? If not, check with the teacher and the suttas to see if what is being taught agrees with them. As your practice deepens and the meditation becomes better, the suttas get easier to understand. This always happens when the teacher is using the suttas as their guide.

**The Hindrances**

Lastly, it is very important for the meditator to recognize whenever the five hindrances" arise. They are:
1. Lust or greed,
2. Hatred or aversion,
3. Sloth and torpor or sleepiness and dullness,

4. Restlessness or remorse, anxiety or scatteredness, and
5. Doubt.

A hindrance is an obstacle or a distraction because it completely blocks your progress during sitting meditation or it can make things difficult during your daily activities. It keeps you from seeing things clearly in the present moment. It also causes you to take an impersonal process, personally.

Whenever these hindrances arise, you identify with them very strongly and you take them personally i.e., "I am sleepy, I am restless, I like and I want, I dislike and I hate, I have doubt". These hindrances completely cloud your mind and stop you from seeing clearly whatever happens in the present moment due to the ego involvement of "I am that".

When you are practicing "fixed absorption concentration' you let go of any distraction and then redirect your mind's attention back to the meditation object. On the other hand, while you are practicing "Tranquil Wisdom Insight Meditation" (TWIM), you let go of the distraction, and this part is exactly the same as the 'fixed absorption concentration', but then, you relax the tightness in the head and feel mind become open, expanded and calm. Now, you smile. Only then do you redirect mind's attention back to the object of meditation.

Over the past fifteen years, the author has developed a training aid to assist the student to practice this technique which is in line with the suttas and which improves mindfulness very much. This is called "The 6R's". The small difference of relaxing mind and feeling it open and calm, changes the whole meditation from a 'fixed absorption concentration' to a more flowing, tranquil kind of awareness, that doesn't go as deep as the absorption types of meditation. As a result, the meditator becomes more in tune with the teachings in the suttas.

In Buddhist meditation, have the questions ever come up, "What is mindfulness (*Sati*), really?"... "Exactly how do you practice being mindful?"... "Can mindfulness really lighten up my perspective and help bring joy, happiness and balance into every aspect of my life?"

If mindfulness is observing how mind's attention moves when a distraction arises and pulls you away from whatever you are doing, then by doing this practice, life becomes easier and more stress free, doesn't it seem like a useful tool to develop?

To clearly understand this connection, you first have to start with a precise definition of Meditation (*Bhāvanā*) and Mindfulness (*Sati*). Seeing this will help you gain a new harmonious perspective (*Samma Ditthi*) of exactly how mind works and teaches the meditator 'HOW' to change old painful habits that cause great suffering into a new way of having a contented, balanced mind. This is the point of all of the Buddha's teachings, isn't it?

Meditation (*Bhāvanā*) is "observing how mind's attention moves moment-to-moment in order to see precisely 'HOW' the impersonal (*anattā*) process of Dependent Origination (*Paṭicca-Samuppāda*) occurs and to completely understand the Four Noble Truths."

Seeing and understanding 'HOW' mind's attention moves from one thing to another and understanding that everything is an impersonal process is what the main thrust is in Buddhist Meditation! This is why Dependent Origination is so important to see and understand. It helps us to develop an impersonal perspective with all arising phenomena and leads you to see for yourself the true nature of all existence.

Why is this important? Because concerning awakening, it has been said by the Blessed One: in Majjhima Nikāya Sutta 28, section 28, *"One who sees Dependent Origination sees the Dhamma; one who sees the Dhamma sees Dependent Origination."*

**What is Mindfulness?**

Mindfulness (*Sati*) is "remembering to observe HOW mind's attention moves moment-to-moment and remembering what to do with any arising phenomena!" Successful meditation needs a highly developed skill of Mindfulness. The 6R's training taught at Dhamma Sukha Meditation Center is a reclaimed ancient guidance system which develops this skill.

The first R is to RECOGNIZE but before we do it, the meditator must remember to use their observation power [mindfulness] for the meditation cycle to start running. Mindfulness is the fuel. It's just like gas for an engine. Without Mindfulness, everything stops!

Being persistent with this practice will relieve suffering of all kinds.

To begin this cycle "smoothly" you must start the engine and have lots of gas (mindfulness) in the tank!

Meditation (*Bhāvanā*) helps you to let go of such difficult delusional states in life as fear, anger, tension, stress, anxiety, depression, sadness, sorrow, fatigue, condemnation, feelings of helplessness or whatever the "catch (attachment) of the day" happens to be. (Delusional means here, taking things that arise personally and identifying with them to be "I", "Me", "Mine" or *"atta"* in Pāli). These states result in suffering that we cause ourselves. This suffering comes from a lack of understanding in how things actually occur.

## The 6R's

The 6R's are steps which evolve into one fluid motion becoming a new wholesome habitual tendency that relieves any dis-ease in mind and body. This cycle begins when MINDFULNESS remembers the 6R's which are:

**RECOGNIZE**
**RELEASE**
**RELAX**
**RE-SMILE**
**RETURN**
**REPEAT**

Development of mindfulness (your observation power) observes each step of the practice cycle. Once you understand what the purpose of mindfulness is, keeping it going all the time is no longer a problem, and this makes the meditation easier to understand, plus, it is much more fun to practice. It becomes a part of happy living and this brings up a smile. Remembering the 6r's leads you to having a wholesome up-lifted mind.

This remembering by mindfulness is very important. Before practicing the 6R's you have to REMEMBER to start the cycle! That's the trick! You have to remember to gas-up the engine, so it can run smoothly!

Then we begin to:

**RECOGNIZE**: Mindfulness remembers how you can recognize and observe any movement of mind's attention from one thing to another. This observation notices any movement of mind's attention away from an object of meditation, such as the breath, sending out *Mettā* or, doing a task in daily life. You will notice a slight tightness or tension sensation as mind's attention barely begins to move toward any arising phenomena.

Pleasant or painful feeling can occur at any one of the six sense doors. Any sight, sound, odor, taste, touch, or thought can cause this pulling sensation to begin. With careful non-judgmental observation, the meditator will notice a slight tightening sensation. RECOGNIZING early movement is vital to successful meditation. You then continue on to;

**RELEASE**: When a feeling or thought arises, you RELEASE it, let it be there without giving anymore attention to it. The content of the distraction is not important at all, but the mechanics of HOW it arose are important! Just let go of any tightness around it; let it be there without placing attention on it. Without attention, the tightness passes away. Mindfulness then reminds you to;

**RELAX**: After releasing the feeling or sensation, and allowing it to be there without trying to control it, there is a subtle, barely noticeable tension within mind/body. This is why the RELAX step ["TRANQUILIZATION" step as stated in the suttas] is being pointed out by the Buddha in his meditation instructions. PLEASE, DON'T SKIP THIS STEP! It would be like not putting oil in a car so the motor can run smoothly. The important Pāli word here is *'pas'sambaya'*. This word specifically means 'to tranquilize' and appears as 'an action verb to be performed' as described in the suttas and is not 'a general kind of relaxing that is included within other release steps found in other kinds of meditation. This point is sometimes mis-understood in translation which then changes the end result!

Without performing this step of relaxation every time in the cycle, the meditator will not experience a close-up view of the ceasing (cessation) of the tension caused by craving or the feeling of relief as the tightness is relaxed. Note that craving always first manifests as a tightness or tension in both one's mind and body. You have a momentary opportunity to see and experience the true nature and relief of cessation of tightness and suffering while performing the RELEASE/RELAX steps.

Mindfulness moves on by remembering to;

**RE-SMILE:** If you have listened to the Dhamma talks at www. dhammasukha.org you might remember hearing about how smiling is an important aspect for the meditation. Learning to smile with mind and raising slightly the corners of the mouth helps mind to be observant, alert and agile. Getting serious, tensing up or frowning causes mind to become heavy and your mindfulness becomes dull and slow. Your insights become more difficult to see, thus slowing down your understanding of Dhamma.

Imagine for a moment, the Bodhisatta resting under the rose apple tree as a young boy. He was not serious and tense when he attained a pleasant abiding [*Jhāna*] and had deep insights with a light mind. Want to see clearly? It's easy!

Just lighten up, have fun exploring and smile! Smiling leads us to a happier more interesting practice. If the meditator forgets to Release/Relax, rather than punishing or criticizing yourself, be kind, re-smile and start again. Keeping up your humor, sense of fun exploration and recycling is important.

After re-smiling, mindfulness recalls the next step.

**RETURN** or **RE-DIRECT:** Gently re-direct mind's attention back to the object of meditation (that is the breath and relaxing, or *Mettā* and relaxing) continuing with a gentle collected mind and use that object as a "home base". In daily life, having been pulled off task, this is where you return your attention back to releasing, relaxing, and re-smiling into the task.

Sometimes people say this practice cycle is simpler than expected! In history, simple things can become a mystery through small changes and omissions! Doing this practice develops better focus on daily tasks with less tension and tightness. Mind becomes more naturally balanced and happy. You become more efficient at whatever you do in life and, actually, you have more fun doing all of the things that used to be a drudgery. Nearing the end of the cycle.

Mindfulness helps with the final remembering to;

**REPEAT**: REPEAT your meditation on your object and keep it going as long as you can and then repeat this entire practice cycle as needed to attain the results the Buddha said could be reached in this lifetime!

Repeating the "6R's cycle" over and over again will eventually replace old habitual suffering as we see clearly for ourselves what suffering actually is; notice the cause of it and how we become involved with the tension and tightness of it; experience how to reach a cessation of that suffering by releasing and relaxing; and discover how we can exercise the direct path to that same cessation of suffering. We achieve this cessation each time we Release an arising feeling, Relax and Resmile. Notice the Relief!

In summary, Mindfulness (*Sati*) is very relevant to Buddhist meditation and daily life. Sharpening your skill of mindfulness is the key to simple and smooth meditation. The process of remembering keeps the six steps of the practice moving. Practicing this meditation as close to the instructions (found in the suttas) as possible will lighten life's experience. A very similar practice was taught to people in the time of the Buddha. It was taught as Right Effort. Within the 6R's we have added a couple more steps to make things a little easier to understand.

The remarkable results of doing the meditation in this way are "immediately effective" for anyone who diligently and ardently embraces these instructions. When you have an attachment arise this practice will eventually dissolve the hindrance, but it does take persistent use of the 6R's to have this happen.

When you practice in this way, because it is found to be so relevant in daily life, it changes your perspective and leads you to a more successful, happy, and peaceful experience. As mindfulness develops, knowledge and wisdom grow naturally as you see HOW things work by witnessing the impersonal process of Dependent Origination.

This leads to a form of happiness the Buddha called "Contentment". Contentment is the by-product of living the Buddhist practice. This meditation leads to balance, equanimity, and the dissolution of fear and other dis-ease. With less fear and dread you find new confidence. Then Loving-kindness, Compassion, Joy, and Equanimity can grow in our lives.

Your degree of success is directly proportional to how well you understand mindfulness, follow the precise instructions, and use the 6R's in both your sitting practice and daily life. This is the way to the end of suffering. It's interesting and fun to practice this way and certainly it helps you smile while changing the world around you in a positive way.

When you are practicing "Tranquil Wisdom Insight Meditation" (TWIM), you do not suppress anything. Suppression means we would push down or push away or not allow certain types of experience. This would temporarily stop hindrances from arising. Instead, when a hindrance arises, you must work to open your mind by seeing clearly *anicca* (impermanence, it wasn't there and now it is), *dukkha* (suffering or un-satisfactoriness, you see that when these distractions arise they are painful), and *anattā* (not taking it personally, seeing the hindrances in the true way as being an impersonal process that you have no control over and not taking these hindrances as "I am that").

You then let go of this obstruction, relax the tightness in the head, calm mind and finally, redirect your craving-free attention back to the practice of 'Mindfulness of Breathing'.

As a result, you begin to see clearly how mind works and this leads to the development of wisdom. Instead of identifying with them, when you allow them and relax, these hindrances, will naturally fade away. Mind becomes more clear and bright. Every time you let go of the ego attachment of "I am that", mind naturally becomes more expanded, alert, and mindful.

Thus, one of the main reasons for this book is to show that whenever you suppress anything, you are not purifying mind, or experiencing things as they truly are. At the time of suppression, you are pushing away or not allowing part of your experience. Thus, mind is contracted and pulls the tension even tighter instead of expanding and opening. As a result, this is not purifying mind of ignorance and craving. You are actually stopping the purification of mind!

It is impossible to experience the unconditioned state of the supramundane *Nibbāna* when one does not let go of everything that arises, and in that way, purify mind of the ego belief of "I am that".

The Buddha never taught suppression of any experience nor did he teach a meditation that causes mind to fix on or become absorbed into the meditation object. Remember, he rejected every form of 'concentration meditation' as not being the correct way. Actually, any kinds of pain, emotional upset, physical discomfort, and even death must be accepted with equanimity, full awareness or strong attention without identifying with these states or taking pain personally.

Real personality change occurs when you open and expand your mind and let go of any kinds of hindrances, pain, suffering and tension even in your daily lives. This means that you open and expand your awareness so that you can observe everything with a silent mind free from tightness and all ego-attachment. You gradually lead a happy and calm life without a lot of mind chatter, especially during your daily activities.

When you practice "concentration meditation", you will feel very comfortable and happy while in the deep meditation. But, when you get out of these exalted stages, your personality remains the same. Old anger, fears, or anxiety remain. This means when the hindrances attack you, you do not recognize them and open your mind and allow the hindrance to be there without taking it personally. Thus, you contract your mind and become even more attached! You might even become prideful and critical! This is because whenever a hindrance arises during the meditation, you let it go and immediately go back to the object of meditation again. You do this without calming and relaxing the tightness caused by the distraction. While in meditation, your mind tends to close or contract and tighten around that experience until mind becomes more deeply 'concentrated'.

As a result, although this suppresses the hindrance, you have not completely let go of the ego-attachment to that distraction. Your mind is also tight and tense because you are not seeing clearly. You are not opening and allowing, but, instead you are closing and fighting with that distraction.

This explains why nowadays meditators complain that they have huge amounts of tension in their head. Actually, if you truly let go of any distraction, there will not ever be any tension in the head. It is as a result of this suppression that there is no real purifying of mind, and thus, personality change does not occur.

**Talking About Words**

Now, we are almost ready for the Ānāpānasati Sutta. But, before we go into that, let's look at some words which have been simplified so that their meanings in the texts become clearer.

For instance,
The word 'rapture' is replaced by 'joy'.
The word 'pleasure' is changed to 'happiness'.
The word 'concentration' is replaced by 'stillness', 'collectedness', or 'unified mind'.
The phrase 'applied and sustained thoughts' is replaced by 'thinking and examining thoughts' which seems to be more immediately understood.
The word 'contemplation' has, in most cases been changed to 'observation'.

When you practice according to the Buddha's instructions, as described here, afterwards, you will be able to confirm your experiences by reading the suttas. As a result, there will arise a better understanding of these profound texts.

One last note: In these few opening chapters, the author has touched on some controversial views about the practices of absorption or fixed concentration (*appanā samādhi*), access concentration (*upacāra samādhi*) and momentary concentration (*khanika samādhi*). Thus, the author would appreciate it very much if the reader finds any mistake; they should indicate the suttas which mentioned these various concentration practices by e-mailing the Author.

When you practice "Tranquil Wisdom Insight Meditation" (TWIM) there is only opening, expanding of mind, and allowing; then relaxing the tightness caused by the hindrance or distraction, before going back to the object of meditation again. This opening and allowing helps you to be more aware of the things which cause pain and suffering so that you can open up and expand even further. With this kind of awareness, there is personality change and only then can you fulfill the Buddha's admonition of "We are the Happy Ones".

# The Ānāpānasati Sutta

## Introductory Section

1] Thus have I heard. On one occasion the Blessed One was living at Savatthi in the Eastern Park, in the Palace of Migara's Mother, together with many very well-known elder disciples— the Venerable Sāriputta, the Venerable Mahā Moggallana, the Venerable Mahā Kassapa, the Venerable Mahā Kaccana, the Venerable Mahā Kotthita, the Venerable Mahā Kappina, the Venerable Cunda, the Venerable Anuruddha, the Venerable Revata, the Venerable Ānanda, and other very well known elder disciples.

2] Now on that occasion elder monks had been teaching and instructing new monks; some elder monks had been teaching and instructing ten new monks, some elder monks had been teaching and instructing twenty... thirty... forty new monks. And the new monks, taught and instructed by the elder monks, had achieved successive stages of high distinction.

3] On that occasion—the Uposatha day of the fifteenth, on the full-moon night of the Pavarana ceremony, [9] The Blessed One was seated in the open surrounded by the 'saṅgha of monks'. Then, surveying the silent 'saṅgha of bhikkhus', he addressed them thus:

4] "Monks, I am content with this progress. My mind is content with this progress. So, arouse still more energy to attain the unattained, to achieve the unachieved, to realize the unrealized. I shall wait here at Savatthi for the Komudi full moon of the fourth month."

The monks can still practice their meditation or make new robes and prepare to go out wandering or teaching the Dhamma to other monks and laypersons during this extra month. The Kaṭhina Ceremony is also held during this month. This is the time for laymen and laywomen to make extra merit by practicing their generosity by giving robes and other requisites to the saṅgha members.

5] The monks of the countryside heard: "The Blessed One will wait there at Savatthi for the Komudi full moon of the fourth month." And the monks of the countryside left in due course for Savatthi to see the Blessed One.

6] And the elder monks still more intensively taught and instructed new monks; some elder monks taught and instructed ten new monks, some elder monks taught and instructed twenty... thirty... forty new monks. And the new monks, taught and instructed by the elder monks, achieved successive stages of high distinction.

7] On that occasion—the Uposatha day of the fifteenth, the full-moon night of the Komudi full moon of the fourth month—the Blessed One was seated in the open surrounded by the 'saṅgha of monks'. Then, surveying the silent 'saṅgha of monks', he addressed them thus:

8] "Monks, this assembly is free from prattle; this assembly is free from chatter.[10] It consists purely of heartwood.

Such is this 'saṅgha of monks', such is this assembly. Such an assembly as is worthy of gifts, worthy of hospitality, worthy of offerings, worthy of reverential salutation, an incomparable field of merit for the world—Such is this assembly. Such an assembly that a small gift given to it becomes great and a great

**gift becomes greater—such is this 'saṅgha of monks', such is this assembly.**

**Such an assembly as is rare for the world to see—such is this 'saṅgha of monks, such is this assembly. Such an assembly as would be worthy journeying many leagues with a travel-bag to see—such is this 'saṅgha of monks', such is this assembly.**

**9] "In this 'saṅgha of monks', there are monks who are Arahats with taints destroyed, who have lived the holy life, done what had to be done, laid down the burden, reached the true goal, destroyed the fetters of being, and are completely liberated through final knowledge—such monks are there in this 'saṅgha of monks'.**

This is the stage where all of the fetters are destroyed such that they will not ever arise anymore.

The ten fetters (saṁyojana) are:

1. Belief in permanent self or soul (sakkāyadiṭṭhi),
2. Doubt in the correct path (vicikicchā),
3. Belief that chanting, or rites and rituals lead one to Nibbāna (sīlabbatapārāmāsa),
4. Lust or greed (kāmarāga),
5. Hatred or aversion (paṭigha),
6. Greed for fine-material existence or immaterial existence (rūparāga),
7. Conceit or pride (arūparāga),
8. Sloth and torpor or sleepiness or dullness of mind (māna),
9. Restlessness or agitation of mind (uddhacca),
10. Ignorance (avijjā).

The final stage of an Arahat is described as follows:
(Taken from the Majjhima Nikāya sutta number 70, section 12.)

**#12]** *"They are the ones who have lived the Holy Life, laid down the burden, reached the true goal, destroyed the fetters of being, and are completely liberated through final knowledge, they have done their work with diligence; they are no longer capable of being negligent"*

Ānāpānasati Sutta:

**10]** **"In this 'sangha of monks' there are monks who, with the destruction of the five lower fetters, are due to reappear spontaneously (in the pure abodes) and there attain final *Nibbāna*, without ever returning from that world—such monks are there in this 'sangha of monks'.**

This stage of sainthood is called *Anāgāmī* where lust and hate no longer even arise in one's mind. The five lower fetters have been destroyed but there is still work to be done.

**11]** **"In this 'sangha of monks there are monks who, with the destruction of three fetters and with the attenuation of lust, hate and delusion, are once-returners, returning once to this world to make an end of suffering—such monks are there in this 'sangha of monks'.**

This stage of sainthood is called being a Sakadāgāmī or once-returner. They have given up the belief in a permanent self, belief that one can attain enlightenment by chanting and practicing rites and rituals, and they have given up doubt in the path. Also, the person who has attained this stage has tremendously weakened lust and hatred, together with all of the other fetters.

**12]** **"In this 'sangha of monks' there are monks who, with the destruction of the three fetters, are stream-enterers, no longer subject to perdition, bound [for deliverance], headed for**

awakening—such monks are there in this 'saṅgha of monks'.

The person who has attained this stage of awakening is called a *Sotāpanna* or stream-enterer. They have given up the three lower fetters mentioned above; they are never going to be reborn in a low existence again. Their lowest rebirth will be as a human being, and the most lives that they will experience before attaining final *Nibbāna*, is seven.

13] "In this 'saṅgha of monks' there are monks who abide devoted to the development of the four foundations of mindfulness [11]—such monks are there in this 'saṅgha of monks'. In this 'saṅgha of monks' there are monks who abide devoted to the four right kinds of strivings (efforts)... to the four bases for spiritual power... to the five faculties... to the five powers... to the seven enlightenment factors... to the Noble Eightfold Path—such monks are there in this 'saṅgha of monks'

The four right kinds of striving, the four bases for spiritual power, the five faculties, the five powers, the seven awakening factors and the Noble Eightfold Path are described in Mahāsakuludayi Sutta, sutta number 77, section 16 of the Majjhima Nikāya. This shows us how to develop wholesome states. (This sutta describes the qualities of Buddha which his disciples repeat to honor, respect, revere and venerate him and live in dependence on him.)
We will now look into the meanings of these terms. The Four Foundations of Mindfulness, the Seven Awakening Factors and the Noble Eightfold Path will be discussed later in the sutta.

### The Four Right Kinds of Striving

"Again Udayin, I have proclaimed to my disciples the way to develop the four right kinds of striving. A monk awakens

**enthusiasm, for the non-arising of unarisen evil unwholesome states, and he makes effort, arouses energy, exerts his mind, and strives."**

Besides enthusiasm, the Pāli word *"chanda"* also means joyful interest or enthusiasm. A mind which points towards a wholesome object like joy has this quality of joyful interest.

Thus, the first right kind of striving is to cultivate a mind that has joyful interest and enthusiasm so that mind becomes clear and free from unwholesome states. Joy grows when mind is smiling and happy during our daily life as well as during meditation. As a result, mind will be uplifted and wholesome at that time. Nowadays, these four kinds of striving are usually called the four right efforts. Some meditation teachers request the meditator to put out strenuous effort to note what is happening in the present moment. But this sutta clearly shows us that this is not that kind of mindfulness.

Mindfulness of joyful interest and enthusiasm, i.e., having a smiling mind leads to a mind which is light, open, accepting, and without any tension. This is the proper definition of right effort and according to the sutta, it actually has nothing to do with noting a phenomena until it goes away.

**"He awakens enthusiasm for the abandoning of arisen evil unwholesome states, and he makes effort, arouses energy, exerts his mind, and strives."**

The second right kind of right striving teaches one to abandon heavy emotional states like anger, sadness, jealousy, anxiety, stress, depression, fear, etc., and replace them with a smiling mind which relaxes away even the subtlest tension. This is the wholesome state of joyful interest and enthusiasm. By cultivating such a smiling mind, one overcomes the ego-identification with these states as being "Mine". A good sense of humor about oneself is a skillful tool to develop when treading the spiritual path.

**"He awakens zeal for the arising of unarisen wholesome states, and he makes effort, arouses energy, exerts his mind, and strives."**

This means seeing that mind brings up joyful interest and enthusiasm when these wholesome states are not in mind. In other words, the cultivation of mindfulness means cultivating joy and a smiling mind. Even when there is a neutral mind that is merely thinking this and that, this is the time to practice smiling in mind and experiencing joyful interest and enthusiasm.

**"He awakens enthusiasm for the continuous, non-disappearance, strengthening, increase, and fulfillment by development of arisen wholesome states, and he makes effort, arouses energy, exerts his mind, and strives. And thereby many disciples of mine abide having reached the consummation and perfection of direct knowledge."**

The fourth right kind of striving refers to a continuous practice, not only during the formal practice of meditation but also during the daily activities.

At one time the author was approached by some questioning students asking: "How can one attain *Nibbāna* by practicing smiling and having joyful interest?" They thought that they had made a very profound statement because they think *Nibbāna* is attained by looking at pain and suffering all of the time. These students are not practicing how to be light and happy as taught by the Buddha. The author replied to them by asking some cross questions: "How can you get to *Nibbāna* without smiling and having joyful interest in your mind?

Isn't joy one of the awakening factors? Didn't the Buddha say 'We are the Happy Ones'?

Here you can see the importance of developing a mind that smiles and has joyful interest. There arises a true change of perspective in your mind when you have joyful interest and a smile. You are not so heavy and grumpy when things become difficult. This is because there is not so much ego-attachment and the meditator can see a situation clearly.

When mind does not smile and has no joyful interest, everything becomes heavy and all mental states and thoughts become depressing. Mind becomes overly serious and takes everything negatively.

For example, let's say that you are very happy and I come along and give you a rose. You might take that rose and admire the color, the shape, and the fragrance. You think, "What a beautiful flower! Just seeing it makes me even happier". But, if you are in a depressed or angry mood and I come along and gave you that same rose, your mind would see the thorns instead. You might even think, "Ugh! This rose is so ugly. I hate it!" At that time, all that is seen is the thorns. But, in actual fact, the rose is the same. The only difference is your mood. Joyful interest and smiling helps to make the world around you a better place to live. This, however, is not to say that we won't go through trials and tribulations. We will! However, the perspective of having joy in mind changes a big problem into a small one.

## The Four Bases for Spiritual Power

"Again, Udayin, I have proclaimed to my disciples the way to develop the four bases for spiritual power. Here a monk develops the basis for spiritual power consisting in composure of mind, due to joy and determined striving."

The first spiritual power refers to **joy**. It is as explained above.

"He develops the basis for spiritual power consisting of collectedness (here meaning stillness) due to energy and determined striving."

This is the second spiritual power **energy**. You cannot slack or become lazy when you are on the Buddha's Path. It takes a lot of energy to stay on the path especially when you realize that this is a lifetime practice! This is talking about the energy that it takes to recognize when your mind is tight and tense, followed by the energy to let go of the thinking and relax the tightness in the head and mind, before coming back to the breath.

"He develops the basis for spiritual power consisting of collectedness (here meaning serenity) due to purity of [i.e. no craving] mind and determined striving."

The third spiritual power refers to the **purity of mind** which is developed when one stays on the object of meditation as long as possible. Whenever a hindrance arises and knocks you out of the meditation, you simply allow the hindrance to be, without getting involved with the thinking mind. You proceed to run the 6R's cycle. That is RECOGNIZING you are not on your object of meditation, RELEASING your distraction by not keeping your attention on it, RELAXING the tension and tightness in your head caused by that distraction, SMILING to lighten up mind and sharpen awareness, and RETURNING to your object of meditation. Then you REPEAT this cycle as needed and you develop this cycle into one flowing motion that mind learns to do.

It doesn't matter how many times mind goes back to that distraction or hindrance. If mind's attention is pulled away, you then run this cycle.

You simply repeat the 6R's, allowing, relaxing, and coming back to the breath and relaxing again. This is the method to purify mind of all defilements and hindrances. Remember, meditation is not about thinking. It's about expanding your understanding mind and awareness into the present moment and then going beyond that to the true expression of loving acceptance. Meditation is the silence when thoughts—with all their images and words have entirely stopped pulling mind's attention away. But meditation is not now, nor, has it ever meant to be 'concentration' in the conventional sense.

'Concentration', the one-pointed or absorption type, contracts mind and is a form of exclusion, a type of cutting off, a suppression of hindrances, a resistance. It is also a kind of conflict. A meditative mind can be very still and composed, and yet, not have exclusion or suppression, or resistance in it. An absorbed concentrated mind cannot meditate according to the Buddhist practice.

**"He develops the basis for spiritual power consisting in collectedness (here meaning composure of mind, or serenity) due to investigation and determined striving."**

The habit of **investigation** of one's experience is a very important aspect of your spiritual growth. When you are caught by a hindrance, a pain, or any distraction, you must be able to see how mind's attention reacts to that particular situation. For example, sleepiness arises while you are meditating. The way to overcome sleepiness is by staying more attentive, with joyful interest, on the object of meditation. You must try to see directly how your mind's attention slips back to the sleepiness.

In other words, you must put more effort and energy into the practice so that you see how things happen. When you notice how mind first starts to be caught by the hindrance, you will let go of it more quickly and not be caught for too long a time.

However, if you are totally caught by sleepiness, it may take some time to overcome this hindrance because this is the last thing mind wants to do! Thus, mind may 'ping pong' back and forth from the meditation object back to the sleepiness. The more light and joyful interest towards how mind's attention works, the more quickly you will let go of the hindrance and begin to meditate again.

Similarly, when pain arises, you do not direct mind's attention into the pain. You can see how mind has resistance to that sensation only when your attention is pulled to the pain. If you start to think about the pain, it will get bigger and more intense. So, first you let go of the thinking mind, which verbalizes about the distraction (pain, hindrance, heavy emotion etc.).

Next, relax mind and release the tight mental knot around the sensation, relax the tightness in the head, calm mind, and then smile before redirecting mind's attention back to the object of meditation. This is done continually until the pain doesn't pull mind's attention to it again.

This is decidedly different from some other meditation

instructions where meditators are told to put their attention into the middle of the pain and note it as 'pain... pain... pain'. All the while, they are trying to see it's true nature and watch it change. But pain, by nature, is repulsive and thus, the meditators have the tendency to tighten and harden mind so that they are able to continue watching the pain. This hardening of mind's attention is never noted by the meditators. This is never seen clearly when it arises. The meditators will eventually develop enough concentration (fixed attention) to be able to overcome the pain. However, this is achieved by suppressing and tightening mind.

You can clearly observe that the spiritual base of investigation of your experience (*Dhamma-vicaya*) is to purify mind by allowing everything that happens in the present moment to be there without trying to fight it, control it, or even disturb it in any way. Loving-acceptance and patience (as defined in the English dictionary means 'non-aversion') of the present moment. This is the way to attain *Nibbāna*. It is not attained by absorption concentration, tightness, or suppression.

**The Five Faculties**

**"Again Udayin, I have proclaimed to my disciples the way to develop the five spiritual faculties. Here a monk develops the faculty of faith which leads to peace, leads to awakening."**

The faculty of **faith** is also called the faculty of **confidence**. As you become interested in letting go of the pain of living, your curiosity becomes stronger. Thus, you begin to look for a meditation teacher. If you are fortunate enough to learn from a competent guide, you will begin to see some slight changes in the way you perceive the world. As you begin to see this through direct practice, your confidence begins to grow. As a result, enthusiasm towards the practice increases so that you will want to practice more!

**"He develops the faculty of <u>energy</u>, which leads to peace, leads to awakening."**

When your confidence grows, you will naturally put more **energy** into your practice. You begin to sit a little longer and mind becomes a little clearer. For the beginner it is recommended to sit not less than 30-45 minutes at a time.

When a sitting is good, please stay with that sitting for as long as it lasts. A good sitting might last for one hour, one hour-ten minutes, or longer. It is good to sit progressively for longer periods of time and not worry about becoming attached to the sitting. The only way you become attached is by the thinking about the meditation instead of doing the meditation in the correct manner. There is nothing wrong in sitting for long periods of time as long as you do not hurt yourself physically and you have enough exercise.

Sitting for one or two or three hours is fine only when you are ready to sit comfortably for such long periods. If you sit in a way which causes pain to arise every time, then you are causing yourself unnecessary physical discomfort. This is not a wise thing to do, because the sitting posture should be comfortable. It is alright if you use a stool or chair, as long as you do not lean too much into anything. Leaning is good for sleeping and dullness, but not for meditating! Thus, the more confidence you have, the more energy you put into your practice. Your enthusiasm will naturally increase as you continue practicing.

**"He develops the faculty of <u>mindfulness</u> which leads to peace, leads to awakening."**

As your energy improves, your awareness and **mindfulness** will naturally become stronger. This is a very natural "non-forced" process. Let's take a look at the mind of an ordinary person, a person like you or me. What you find is a grasshopper mind, a butterfly mind, or one could also say, a mad monkey mind. It is always moving, ever-jumping around. It changes its fantasies and impulses at every moment.

Mind's attention is prey for all stimuli and its own emotional reaction to them. This is actually a reaction that is mostly reacting to conditions the way you always act when a certain stimuli arises. It is a chain of linked associations, hopes, fears, memories, fantasies, or regrets that are streaming constantly through mind. These are triggered by memories of the outside world.

Mind's attention is blindly moving, never-stopping, never-satisfied in its search for pleasure and satisfaction. It is no wonder that mind becomes so crazy and filled with un-satisfactoriness and was described by the early monks as a restless mad monkey swinging from branch-to-branch in the quest for satisfying fruit through the endless jungle of conditional events.

Thus, when you first begin to meditate, mind's attention naturally runs all over the place and it stays away from the object of meditation for a long time. Sometimes it even takes two or three minutes before you are able to recognize that it is being pulled away and then, you gently let it go, relax the tension in the head, calm mind, smile and re-direct mind's attention back to the breath and relaxing.

When this happens, this is only natural, because mind is used to running wherever it likes to go. When it does happen, please don't criticize yourself or beat yourself up because mind's attention is so unruly. Instead, release the distraction, relax, smile as you return back to the object of meditation and continue on.

As your practice develops and you are able to recognize and let go more quickly, your mindfulness gradually becomes sharper. Mind might only stay away from the breath and relaxing for one minute before recognizing that it is not on the breath and relaxing. It then lets go, relaxes, smiles, and comes back to the breath and relaxes again.

At this time mind's attention begins to stay on the breath and relaxing for longer periods of time, perhaps, as long as thirty seconds, before it goes off again. However, you are now becoming better at seeing when mind's attention goes away. Your mindfulness becomes sharper and you are able to recognize what mind is doing. Thus, when your confidence becomes better, energy improves, and as a result, the alertness of mind naturally develops and this is sharpening your mindfulness. One of the most important parts of this meditation is to realize that the 'breath and relaxing' should be your re-centering point for each cycle.

**"He develops the faculty of <u>collectedness</u> or stillness, which leads to peace, leads to awakening."**

When your mindfulness of the present moment improves, mind will naturally stay on the object of meditation for much longer periods of time. Most people would describe this as 'concentration' but this is not an accurate description because this is not that kind of concentration. Mind is not absorbed into or fixed on just the breath. Instead, it is very still, relaxed, composed and stays on the breath and relaxing very well. Remember that the breath is the reminder for the RELAX step and that is very important.

At this time a strong feeling of joy arises and the body becomes very light and this feels like floating. When joy fades away, a powerful feeling of tranquility, equanimity, and comfort arises. Due to your sharp awareness, you do not become involved with these feelings. But if you begin to think or internally verbalize about how nice this state is, and how much you like it, you will lose that state and sleepiness very often comes into mind. This is because you are caught by the attachment to those feelings (craving and clinging) and it slips off the object without coming back to the breath and relaxing.

Mindfulness fades away when you start to think or internally verbalize about things and you become involved in wanting to control these things and thoughts. This also happens when you crave for the experience of joy and tranquility to arise. This desire makes mind try too hard so that it can't get back to that experience!. But when you try harder and put in more energy, the restlessness becomes bigger. Often times, you will put even more energy into overcoming this hindrance when what is really needed is to put in less energy and relax and smile more. Turn your meditation into a fun game to play with instead of making the hindrance an enemy to fight with.

These arising combinations of hindrances will stop all spiritual practice from occurring because the desire for things to be in a particular way (craving) makes all the spiritual development fade away. Therefore, you must be more mindful of the thoughts about these pleasant abidings.

As your confidence and smiling increases, your energy grows naturally. This improves your mindfulness which enables the collectedness and stillness of mind to become stronger and last longer.

**"A monk develops the faculty of <u>wisdom</u> (or understanding of how Dependent Origination occurs), which leads to peace,**

**leads to awakening . And thereby many disciples of mine abide having reached the consummation and perfection of direct knowledge."**

As your mind becomes more calm and still, you are able to see the true nature of things. This development of wisdom or intelligence is gained by personally seeing things arise and pass away by themselves. For instance, even while you are sitting in a *Jhāna* [a meditation stage of understanding] you see how joy arises. It is there for a while, then fades away. You then see how tranquility and happiness arise. You are there for a while and then, they fade away. You are able to see the true nature of impermanence, even in the beginning of your practice, by observing thoughts arising and passing away.

You begin to observe feeling and emotions arising and passing away. You will also notice that these things that arise and pass away are un-satisfactory and these feelings and emotions are a form of suffering, especially when they don't behave in the way you want them to. When you see how truly un-satisfactory this process is, you can then clearly see that it is an "impersonal process" (*anattā*). No one controls the appearance and disappearance of these things.

Even while in *Jhāna* [a meditation stage of understanding] you have no real control over joy arising because joy arises when the conditions are right for it to come up. At the same time, you simply cannot force joy to stay because it will fade away when the conditions are right. Whatever arises, passes away.

This causes more un-satisfactoriness to arise, because joy is such a nice feeling! In this way, you are able to see the characteristics of existence very clearly, i.e. *anicca* (impermanence), *dukkha* (suffering), and the impersonal nature of these things (*anattā*).

This is how to develop wisdom which gradually leads us to the seeing of Dependent Origination both arising and ceasing (that is, seeing and realizing The Four Noble Truths). An interesting observation found in the **Vinaya** is that *you can see the three characteristics of existence without ever seeing the links of Dependent Origination, but you can never see the links of Dependent Origination without seeing the three characteristics of existence (i.e., impermanence, suffering and the impersonal nature of everything) at the same time.* We will discuss this in more detail at a later time.


**The Five Powers**


"Again Udayin, I have proclaimed to my disciples the way to develop the Five Spiritual Powers.

Here a monk develops the Power of Faith, which leads to peace, leads to awakening.

He develops the Power of Energy, which leads to peace, leads to awakening.

He develops the Power of Mindfulness, which leads to peace, leads to awakening.

He develops the Power of Collectedness, which leads to peace, and leads to awakening.

He develops the Power of Wisdom (which means seeing and understanding the links of Dependent Origination), which leads to peace, and leads to awakening.

And thereby many disciples of mine abide having reached the

**consummation and perfection of direct knowledge."**

These are the same as the five faculties but, they are called **powers** because of their ability to purify mind and make it wholesome and clean.

We will now continue with the Ānāpānasati Sutta.

**14] "In this sangha of monks there are monks who abide devoted to the development of loving-kindness ... of compassion ... of joy ... of equanimity ... of the meditation of foulness ... of the perception of impermanence—such monks are there in this sangha of monks. In this sangha of monks there are monks who abide devoted to the development of mindfulness of breathing.**

Loving-kindness, Compassion, Joy and Equanimity are known as the Four "*Brahmā Vihāras*" or the Four Boundless states of mind, or the Limitless or Immeasurable states of mind. This is because there are no boundaries or limitations on mind when they are practiced.

The meditation of foulness is suitable for those who have a strong affinity for lust arising in their minds. It is practiced by reflecting on the elements and the disgusting nature of our body parts. For example, when you look at a beautiful person and thoughts of lust arise, you can imagine how desirable that person would be if all of their body parts were to be turned inside-out! Will your mind then think, "Oh! what a lovely intestine or liver!" or "Wow! What beautiful bile, pus and phlegm that person has!" How much lust is there in mind at that time? Thus, this meditation helps people with a lustful personality to come more into balance.

The perception of impermanence does not actually refer to sitting down and thinking about how everything changes. (Remember, "Tranquil Wisdom Insight Meditation" (TWIM) is about seeing with a silent and spacious mind). It is referring to the meditation states of "infinite space" and "infinite consciousness" where mind sees just how fleeting these mental and physical phenomenon truly are and you realize just how unsatisfactory this is. Plus, the biggest insight is when you realize all states of existence are just a part of an impersonal process. In other words, you see and understand that there is no controller and that there is no self-making these things to arise. They arise by themselves. They are there for a brief moment and they go away without you having any control over what happens.

We will now proceed to the next section of the sutta which speaks about "Mindfulness of Breathing".

## Mindfulness of Breathing

15] **"Monks, when mindfulness of breathing is developed and cultivated, it is of great fruit and great benefit. When Mindfulness of Breathing is developed and cultivated, it fulfills the "Four Foundations of Mindfulness". When the "Four Foundations of Mindfulness" are developed and cultivated, they fulfill the "Seven Awakening Factors". When the "Seven Awakening Factors" are developed and cultivated, they fulfill true knowledge and deliverance.**

Please observe that the "Four Foundations of Mindfulness" are in this sutta and they are fulfilled through the practice of *Jhāna* and "Tranquil Wisdom Insight Meditation" (TWIM) which lead to wise meditative states of mind.

This is decidedly different from the current theory that you can't observe the "Four Foundations of Mindfulness" while experiencing *Jhānas* [meditative stages of understanding].

The Buddha only taught one kind of meditation and that is serenity/insight or tranquility/insight meditation. That is *Samatha/Vipassanā* meditation or you can say he taught *Samādhi* which literally means "Tranquil Wisdom Insight Meditation" (TWIM).

**16] And how, monks, is mindfulness of breathing developed and cultivated, so that it is of great fruit and great benefit?**

**17] "Here a monk, gone to the forest or to the root of a tree or an empty hut, sits down; having folded his legs crosswise, set his body erect, and established mindfulness in front of him, ever mindful he breathes in, mindful he breathes out.**

The phrase **"gone to the forest or to the root of a tree or an empty hut"** means that you go to a reasonably quiet place where there will be few distractions while learning the meditation. A suitable location would be a place that is away from road noises, loud and persistent music or sounds of people, as well as animals.

The thing that happens with many absorption concentration practitioners is that even the smallest sound turns into a "thorn in their side". This occurs because concentration is out of balance with your mindfulness. Many students complain about a fan being on and how it makes noise, or when someone opens and shuts a door. The absorption practitioner will jump because the noise kind of shocks them. Again, this occurs because the meditators mindfulness is weak and their concentration is out of balance. This is one of the disadvantages of doing absorption concentration.

During the time of the Buddha, most people sat on floor. Hence, the phrase "**sits down; having folded his legs crosswise, sets his body erect**". But today, sitting on the floor can be very painful and a trying experience because people mostly sit on chairs, stools, or couches. If you want to sit on the floor, it may help if you sit on a cushion high enough so there is no pain in your back or knees.

In actual fact, it is far more important to observe what is happening in mind than it is to sit with uncomfortable or painful sensations. Remember that there is no magic in sitting on the floor. The magic comes from a clear, calm mind that has fun watching how mind's attention moves from one thing to another and learning to 6R any distraction and gently be at ease, as much as possible. Thus, if sitting on the floor is a very painful experience, then, it is alright to sit on a stool or a chair.

However, if you do sit on a chair, there is an extremely important factor to consider. You need to sit without leaning hard against the back of the chair. Leaning is good for sleeping but not for meditation! **"Sets his body erect"** means you sit with a nicely straight back which is not rigid and uncomfortable. A nicely straight back has all of the vertebrae stacked one upon another. This is to ensure that energy can flow up and down the back without any blockages. Leaning into a chair can stop the energy flow and can cause sleepiness to arise. Thus, please do not lean against anything when sitting. Very often, when you first start out, your back is not used to being straight and some of the muscles can rebel and complain. However, with patience and perseverance, these unused muscles will gradually adjust and they will strengthen.

There is another important aspect to sitting meditation. You must not move! You must **sit without moving the body for any reason**. Please do not wiggle the toes or fingers or move the hands to rub or scratch or change the posture in any way until after the sitting is over. Any movement breaks the continuity of the practice and this can cause you to have to start all over again.

Some meditation teachers tell their students that it is quite alright to move as long as they are "mindful". But if the students are truly mindful, they would be able to watch mind and its dislike of the sensations and then, let go of the sensation and relax mind around them. Thus, there would be no reason to move!

Mindfulness also means to lovingly-accept what is happening in the present moment, without trying to control, resist or change it. To be truly mindful means to open up and allow whatever presents itself in the present moment. While sitting, if you move, this means that you are not being mindful at that time. When you "give in" to the desire to move, you are identifying with that desire and there is no mindfulness at that time .

Thus, when you are ready and begin to meditate, you must remain still and keep relaxing mind whenever there is a distraction. To sit as still as a Buddha image is the best! Actually the only allowable movement during meditation is to straighten the back when it starts to curve or slump, as long as it is not done too often.

The phrase **"establishing mindfulness in front of him"** means that you put aside all other worldly affairs and involvement with sensual pleasures. Then you softly close your eyes and whenever there is a distracting sound, smell, taste, sensation, or thought, you are aware of that and simply let it go. You then relax the tightness in your head, smile and redirect mind's attention back to the object of meditation and relax.

**"Ever mindful he breathes in, mindful he breathes out."**

This tells us the way to practice mindfulness of breathing. Being **aware of the breath** means to know when you are experiencing the in-breath, then relaxing, and to know when you are experiencing the out-breath and relaxing. You use the breath as a reminder to relax on both the in and out-breath. It simply means to open up your awareness and to be attentive to the breath as much as possible and at the same time, relax the tightness in the head (this will be explained more thoroughly in a little while).

**Meditation Instructions**

18] **"Breathing in long, he understands: 'I breathe in long'; or breathing out long, he understands: 'I breathe out long.' Breathing in short, he understands: 'I breathe in short'; or breathing out short he understands 'I breathe out short'.**

The words **"he understands"** is emphasized to show that you do not focus with strong attention on the breath to the exclusion of everything else. You merely 'understand' what the breath is doing in the present moment. That's all there is to this! You simply know when you breathe in long or short! There is no controlling of the breath at any time. Instead, there is only understanding of what you are doing in the present moment. If you try to "over-focus" or "concentrate" on the breath to the exclusion of anything else, you will develop a headache due to this "wrong concentration".

Whenever you hold tightly onto the meditation object and try to force mind to "concentrate" or push away distractions, the head will develop a very tight and painful tension. This tightness or tension in the head also occurs when the meditator attempts to control the sitting by throwing down any distracting thoughts and feelings and quickly rushing back to the meditation object. This happens with 'momentary concentration' as well as any other kind of 'absorption concentration' technique. This doesn't happen when you relax on the in-breath and on the out-breath.

Many meditation teachers tell their students to put their attention right in the middle of the sensation and see its true nature. This will cause a few different things to occur.

Firstly, you will develop a stronger pain and this becomes a distraction instead of an investigation. It is because these meditation teachers tell their students to stay with that pain until it goes away. Unfortunately, this can take an unbelievably long time. In addition, you naturally need to tighten and toughen mind in order to observe the sensation.

Actually, this tightening and toughening of mind is not being mindful. You begin to develop a mind that hardens itself when pain arises. It is only natural for this to happen as it takes a lot of courage and fortitude to watch pain in this way. At that time, a type of aversion is naturally developed and this hardening of mind is not being noticed as *anicca*, *dukkha*, *anattā* or the links of Dependent Origination and you are not noticing the craving which is this tightening of mind and body.

Consequently, even when you are not meditating, this suppression can cause personality hardening, and that causes true problems to arise. Without the relax step, mind has a tendency to become critical and judgmental and the personality development of the meditator becomes hard.

Many people say they need to do a Loving-kindness retreat after doing other types of meditation because they discovered that they do and say things in daily life which are not so nice to other people. When this happens, there appears a question, "Is this really a type of meditation technique which leads to my happiness and to the happiness of others?" If the answer is yes, then why do I need to practice another form of meditation to balance my thinking?"

Eventually you are able to suppress this aversion by practicing 'concentration', which is considered to be the "correct method" by most meditation teachers. But the method taught by the Buddha was never to suppress anything. His method was to keep mind open and relaxed and to allow everything that arises in the present moment.

Thus, whenever a painful sensation arises in the body, you first recognize that mind's attention has gone to the sensation and you begin to think about that feeling. You then let go of any thoughts about that sensation, open mind and let go of the tight mental fist that is wrapped around the sensation, or you can let the sensation be there by itself without any mental resistance or aversion to it. This is done by telling yourself, "Never mind, it is alright for this pain to be there."

Next, relax the tightness in the head ... feel mind expand and become calm ... then smile and re-direct mind's attention back to the object of meditation i.e. the breath and relaxing on both the in and out-breath.

If you get caught by thinking about the sensation or pain, the sensation will get bigger and become more intense. Eventually, you can't stand it anymore and you feel like you have to move. This thinking or internal verbalizing about the sensation and wishing it would go away, is the 'ego identification' and the very beginning of craving and clinging. This getting involved with, ... trying to control, ... fighting with the sensation, ... resisting the sensation etc., is only fighting with the Dhamma, which is the Truth of the present moment.

Whenever you fight and try to control or harden mind to the "Dhamma of the present moment", you cause yourself undue suffering and pain. Another way of fighting with the Dhamma is by taking the sensation personally and trying to control feeling with your thoughts. This worsens the pain and, as a result, it hurts even more. Thus, you must learn to open and lovingly-accept the present moment without that 'ego-identification' and the thinking or internal verbalization about it, or taking it as "I am that".

By letting go and relaxing, then smiling, this is how you gain calmness and collectedness of mind as well as equanimity, full awareness, and mindfulness. The Buddha taught us three kinds of actions while meditating or during our daily activities. They are,

"Love Where We Are At...
Love What We Are Doing in the Present Moment...
and Love Who We Are With".

These simple explanations allow you to be completely accepting of the present moment. "To Love Where We Are At" means to accept the fact that when you are sitting in meditation, things are not always like you want them to be.

"To Love What We Are Doing" means to open up mind and allow whatever arises in the present moment to present itself without our getting attached to it (craving) or criticizing ourselves for not being as good as we think we should be.

A good acronym for this is **"DROPSS"** which means "Don't Resist Or Push. Soften and Smile". Whatever arises, do not resist or push. Just soften into it and smile, open mind and accept it. In other words **"Love What We Are Doing"**.

**"To Love Who We Are With"**, means to love yourself enough so that you see and let go of all kinds of attachments which cause pain to arise in your body and mind.

The recognition that you cause your own suffering is a major realization. When you truly love yourself, you will see the pain and sorrow and lovingly let it go, then relax and smile. This is done by letting go of the thinking about. Thus, you will eventually let go of the attachment (craving) and the ego identification with it.

**"He trains thus: 'I shall breathe in experiencing the whole body';**
**he trains thus 'I shall breathe out experiencing the whole body";**

This part of the sutta means that you know when the breath is starting and stopping on the in-breath, then relax. You don't have to over-focus mind or 'concentrate' on the breath, or take this breathing as the object of extreme 'absorption concentration'. You simply know what the breath is doing in the present moment and relax on both the in and out-breath. Your mindfulness is sharp enough to know what the breath and relaxing is doing at all times, without controlling the breath in any way.

Just let the breath and relaxing become a natural process!

**"He trains thus: 'I shall breathe in tranquilizing the bodily formation';**
**he trains thus: 'I shall breathe out tranquilizing the bodily formation'."**

This simple statement is the **most important part** of the meditation instructions. It instructs you to notice the tightness which arises in the head with every arising of a consciousness and to relax that tightness while on the in-breath and out-breath. Then you feel your mind open up, expand, relax, become tranquil. and then you smile.

This process occurs because there is a membrane that is wrapped around the brain called the "meninges". This membrane tightens every time a thought, feeling, or sensation arises. Every time you see that mind is distracted away from the breath and relaxing, you simply let go of the distraction by not keeping mind's attention on it, then relax the tightness in the head or brain, feel mind become open and expanded. Feel it become relaxed, calm and clear.

Next, you softly smile and re-direct mind's attention back to the breath. On the in-breath relax, feel it expand and become calm. On the out-breath relax, feel the meninges expand, feel mind become alert, and pure. In this way the tension in the head (meninges, brain) and mind gently goes away.

For example, when a thought arises, just let the thought go. Don't continue thinking, even if you are in mid-sentence. Just softly let go of the thought. If the distraction is a sensation, firstly open mind and let go of the aversion to the sensation and relax the tightness caused by that distraction. Then feel open and expand before smiling and then re-direct mind's attention back to the breath and relaxing. This opening up, relaxing and letting go of the tightness in the head is actually letting go of the subtle 'ego identification' (craving) which attaches itself to everything as it arises.

Thus, in this way, when you let go of this tension, you are actually letting go of all craving and ignorance which causes rebirth. This is the actual experience of the "Third Noble Truth" or the cessation of suffering.

Many times a teacher of 'absorption concentration' will tell their students that this last part of the instructions means that you become tranquil when you focus mind's attention just on the breath. But, this is not the way this is to be read. The Pāli presents us with the word "pas-sambaya". This word is interesting because it can be a verb, an adverb, a noun, or an adjective. Words which preceed it or follow it change the meaning of this word. The words before this state "He trains thus:". This means that this Pāli word is an "action verb". This makes sense because you are relaxing (letting go of subtle craving) in the body and mind on both the in and out-breaths.

When you follow this sutta's instructions, this small step of relaxing in the instructions actually says that when you meditate, you are not strongly focusing just on the breath itself to the exclusion of everything else. You are using the breath to remind yourself to relax on both the in and out- breaths. This changes the entire meditation moving it away from "absorption concentration" and instead, developing the "Tranquil Wisdom Insight Meditation" (TWIM)!

When the meditation instructions here are followed closely, there will be no 'sign or *nimitta*' arising in mind. A *nimitta* is a kind of mind-made object, which arises when one is practicing 'absorption concentration meditation'. In the practice of TWIM, the Mind naturally becomes calm and your understanding of HOW mind's attention actually moves continues to develop. This also means that you will be able to discern how the links of Dependent Origination occur and this is where deep insights and understanding really happen.

You need not "try" to force mind to stay on the object of meditation through strong concentration which can cause tension and pain (craving) in the head and body. Eventually you begin to realize the true nature of all phenomenon as being impermanent (*anicca*), unsatisfactory (*dukkha*), and not-self (*anattā*) as well as beginning to see for yourself how the impersonal process of Dependent Origination occurs.

Thus, when you practice "Tranquil Wisdom Insight Meditation" (TWIM), you are aware of the in-breath and at the same time, the relaxation of the tension caused by craving in your head because of the tightening of the meninges, the membrane around the brain, and you feel this tightening in your mind as well. You are also aware of the out-breath and again, at the same time, the relaxation of the tension in the head and mind.

Please use the breath as your reminder to relax all tightness because then you are letting go of the craving, which always manifests as tension and tightness in both mind and body.

This is actually an incredibly easy practice and a simple way to develop mind. It is alright if you happen to miss one in-breath or one out-breath at first. You should not put unnecessary pressure on yourself or criticize yourself. This might cause you to think how difficult this practice is. It does take some getting used to before your practice becomes proficient. Thus, if you occasionally miss the in-breath and relaxing, or, an out-breath and relaxing, just let it go and catch the next in-breath or out-breath. Simple and easy, isn't it?

At first, the breath may seem to be very fast and difficult to notice. However, as you continue with your practice, the meditation becomes easier and you will not miss the in-breath and relaxing or the out-breath and relaxing that much. After all, this is a gradual training. There is no need to put undue pressure on yourself, so, have fun and smile more. This is the way to gain the fastest results. Please remember that the Buddha teaches us to have a happy wholesome uplifted mind all of the time! Simply relax into the meditation and smile. Smiling is a way to have an alert uplifted mind!

When you practice "Tranquil Wisdom Insight Meditation" (TWIM), the breath does not become subtle and difficult to observe. If this happens, then the meditator is 'concentrating' too much on the breath and not smiling enough. Also, the tightness in the head is not relaxed enough. If the breath seems to disappear again, the meditator is focusing their 'concentration' and not tranquilizing mind enough.

The *Jhānas* (meditation stages of understanding) will appear by themselves as mind becomes calm and peaceful. You do not have to push, force, or 'concentrate with a fixed mind'. Actually, the Buddha taught this most natural form of meditation to work for every type of personality or individual.

**19] "He trains thus: 'I shall breathe in experiencing joy'; He trains thus: 'I shall breathe out experiencing joy'."**

This refers to the attainment of the first two *Jhānas* (meditation stages of understanding). The description of these stages is a set formula that is repeated many times in the suttas.[12] We will now look into the description of these first two *Jhānas*:

**Here, quite secluded from sensual pleasures, ...**

When you start your meditation session, you first close your eyes. This is being secluded from the sensual pleasure of seeing. Whenever a sound distracts mind, the instructions are to let the sound be there by itself, without thinking about whether you like the sound or not. Simply let the sound go. Let go of the mental fist around the sound. Relax the craving or tightness in the head and feel mind become calm and at ease. Now smile and redirect (happy) mind's attention back to the object of meditation, i.e., the breath. Relax the tightness in the head, feel mind open up, expand, and become tranquil. Smile and on the in-breath, relax the tightness in the head on the out-breath, feel mind become alert, peaceful, and pure because there is no more craving in it. You stay with the breath and relax the tension in mind until the next distraction appears by itself.

As a meditator you do this with smelling, tasting, bodily sensations, and thoughts or any kind of sensual pleasure which distracts mind's attention away from the breath and relaxing.

Whenever there is a distraction at one of the sense-doors you simply and softly let it go, relax that mental fist around the distraction, relax the tightness in the head, feel mind expand, and redirect mind's attention back to the breath and relaxing again. It doesn't matter how many times the sensual pleasure arises. You have to allow it to be there every time it arises. Just remember to let it go, relax the tightness in the head, feel mind expand and smile, then come back to the breath and relaxing.

**secluded from unwholesome states...**

When mind's attention is distracted from the breath and relaxing, and it begins to think about a feeling that arises, then there is a tendency for mind to like or dislike that feeling. This thinking about and trying to control feeling by thinking about what arises, causes the feeling to get bigger and more intense. Thus, more pain arises.

**Five Aggregates**

This psycho-physical process is made up of five different

aggregates which are affected by craving and clinging. The meditator has a physical **body, feeling** (both mental and physical), **perception** (a process of naming things), **thoughts,** and **consciousness.** Knowing this, you can clearly see that feeling is one thing and thoughts are another.

Unfortunately, all of us have developed the habit of trying to think feeling away. This only makes the feeling bigger and more intense. As a result, more pain and suffering arise.

When you practice the Buddha's meditation method, you begin to understand and let go of this old habit of thinking the feeling. Thus, when a feeling arises, no matter whether it is physical or emotional, first, let go of any thoughts about the feeling and relax the tightness in your head caused by that movement of mind's attention.

Next, let go of that tight mental hold around that feeling. Now relax the tightness in the head and feel mind expand. Notice it becomes calm and tranquil. Next, smile and redirect mind's attention back to the breath and relaxing.

When you do this, you are seeing the true nature of that feeling: It wasn't there. Then, it arose by itself, i.e. this is change or impermanence. You certainly do not request for this incredibly painful sensation to arise, nor do you ask at that time to feel angry, sad, fearful, depressed, doubtful or whatever the "catch of the day" happens to be.

A feeling arises by itself, without your desire for it to arise. They last as long as they last. The more you try to control, fight with, or push away a feeling or you try to think the feeling away, the longer it stays and becomes much bigger and extra intense.

This is because whenever you want to control a feeling, you are identifying with that sensation or emotion as being yours personally (craving)! You tend to think about how much it hurts, where it came from, why it has to bother you now? "Oh! I hate that feeling and I want it to go away."

Every thought about the feeling is the ego-identification (which is craving and then clinging) with that feeling. Every time you try to resist what is happening in the present moment, you are fighting with the "Dhamma of the Present Moment". You are fighting with the Truth!

When a painful or even a pleasant feeling arises, the Truth is—it is there. Any resistance, trying to control it, wishing it away with thoughts, or fighting that feeling in any way, only causes more suffering to arise. Actually whenever a feeling arises, you open mind, let go of the want to control, lovingly accept the fact that this feeling is there, and relax and smile—allow it to be there by itself.

"Don't Resist Or Push: Soften and Smile". This **DROPSS** is the key to having an accepting open mind which later develops into equanimity. Any slight resistance or tightness means that there is some craving or ego-identification still attached to it.

Let's say that a friend or a boss came up and scolded you in the early morning after you went to work. What happened to your mind? If you were like most people—you would have scolded them back because you were angry and ready to fight back. When the friend or boss went away, what did you think about? What you said? What your friend, or boss said? What you should have said? "I'm right for feeling the way I do and for what I said. They are wrong for what they said and did." And so it goes on in your mind. This feeling of anger is strong and there were thoughts which were attached to that feeling.

After a little while you distract yourself with some other activities. But the anger is still there and if someone comes to talk to you, chances are good that you will complain about your other friend or boss who scolded you.

So, at that time you are giving your dissatisfaction and anger to someone else and that affects them in a negative way. At different times during the day, these feelings and the thoughts that are attached to them arise. As a matter of fact, these thoughts are just like they were recorded on a cassette tape with a permanent loop going around and around.

They come back in the same order and with exactly the same words. After the end of the day you would have distracted yourself so much that this feeling doesn't come up so often. Then comes the time to sit in meditation and purify mind. But what arises? This feeling of anger, and the associated thoughts come up! Thus, here we go again.

But this time, you 6R as you let go of getting involved with those feelings and thoughts, you begin to relax. Seeing that these thoughts cause the feeling to grow, you then begin to soften mind's attention. "Never mind! It just isn't that important." You Soften... "Let it be"... open mind and let go of that tight mental knot around these thoughts and gently relax the tightness in your head. You let go of the aversion to the feeling and you feel mind begin to relax, then expand, become calm, and you smile, and then redirect mind's attention back to the breath and relaxing. What a relief!

Now gently go back to the breath and, on the in-breath relax the tightness in the head; on the out-breath relax the tightness in the head. Always you are feeling mind open up, expand, and become tranquil, and then you smile.

Then, the anger comes up again, and so, again you do the same thing. You let it be there by itself without getting involved with the thinking about it... open and relax the mental hold on it... relax the tightness in the head... smile... softly re-direct mind's attention back to the breath and relaxing again. This is the process of the 6R's.

It doesn't matter how many times mind's attention goes back to that feeling of anger. It is treated in the same way every time. You are not taking that feeling personally when you let the feeling be there by itself and relax.

Thus, there is no ego-identification (craving or clinging) with that feeling. This is seeing the true nature of that feeling, isn't it? The feeling wasn't there before, but now it is. This is seeing impermanence. When that feeling arises, it takes away the tranquility and peace. That is definitely painful, a true form of suffering. When you allow the feeling to be there by itself without getting involved or thinking about it and you open your mind and relax the tightness away and smile, you are experiencing the impersonal nature (*anattā*) at that time.

Thus, when you practice "Tranquil Wisdom Insight Meditation" (TWIM), you continually experience the Three Characteristics of Existence: impermanence, suffering, and the impersonal nature of everything (*anicca, dukkha, anattā*).

As you continue to relax mind's attention and let go of any distraction, attachment (craving) becomes smaller and weaker. Finally it doesn't have enough strength to arise anymore. When this happens, mind becomes filled with relief and joy arises.

Letting go of attachment (craving) means you become secluded from unwholesome states. When you let go and joy arises, it lasts for a period of time. After that, mind becomes very tranquil and happy (sukha). Now, you will experience a mind which stays on the object of meditation very easily. When this is done repeatedly, mind will naturally become calm and collected by itself. At that time, you begin to develop some equanimity and balance of mind.

**"The monk enters upon and abides in the first Jhāna (meditation stage), which is accompanied by thinking and examining thought, with joy and happiness born of seclusion."**

All of these different factors make up what is commonly called the first Jhāna (meditation stage of understanding). At that time there can still exist some very small wandering thoughts. If mind wanders away from the breath and relaxing, you can easily let that distraction go and relax mind, then smile. The wandering thoughts are noticed very quickly.

Simply let go. Relax the tightness and smile before coming back to the breath and relaxing. Some meditation teachers call this 'access concentration'. But actually they are looking at things from the viewpoint of "concentration meditation" and not "Tranquil Wisdom Insight Meditation" (TWIM).

Thinking and examining thought are descriptions of the thinking mind and discursive thinking (wandering thoughts). Some translations call this initial and sustained thought, thinking and pondering.

There can still be directed thoughts in each one of the different Jhānas (meditation stages of understanding). The difference between directed thought and wandering thoughts is: Directed thought is about what is happening to you in the present moment. With wandering thoughts, you think about what happened in the past or what will happen in the future, or daydream about what you would like to see.

Observation thoughts are a little different. For instance, 'mind feels very happy right now', 'mind is very calm', 'body feels very still and peaceful right now', etc. This is another way of looking at examining thought.

Thinking thought is mind that notices when mind's attention is distracted and brings the attention back to the breath and relaxing. Examining thought is mind that stays on the breath and relaxing without slipping away again and it also has the thoughts of what is happening in the present moment.

When mind's attention begins to stay on the object of meditation for longer and longer periods of time, relief and joy will become quite strong. You will naturally feel like smiling because the joy is such a pleasurable feeling in both mind and body.

At that time, the body and the mind feel very light until it is almost like floating. This is quite a pleasant experience. Some meditation teachers tell their students that when joy arises, "Don't Be Attached!" So, these students become fearful of that joy and try to push it away so that they won't possibly have the chance to become attached.

However, this is not the correct thing to do because it doesn't matter what kind of feeling arises, either pleasurable, painful, or neutral, your job is to see that mind stays on the breath and relaxing and allow those feelings to be there by themselves.

If mind's attention is pulled away by a feeling, simply let it be there by itself and relax the tightness in the head, feel mind open and expand, then go back to the breath. Attachment or "craving" comes from personally getting involved with liking or disliking what arises in the present moment. "Clinging" is the thinking mind where concepts, opinions, ideas, and the story about why you like or dislike that feeling arises. You will not become attached when you allow whatever arises to be there by itself, relax and smile, and then come back to the object of meditation.

After the joy fades away, mind will become very calm, peaceful and comfortable. It is this comfortable and tranquil feeling that is called **"happiness born of seclusion"**.

At first, you can sit in this stage of meditation for 5 or 6 minutes. You can do this for longer periods as mind becomes quieter. This is the first *Jhāna* (meditation stage of understanding) and it will arise when you have let go of sensual pleasure for a period of time, and have also let go of unwholesome habits or states of mind (the craving and clinging) which stop the meditator from having a mind without distractions in it.

Once you have experienced this state of calm, you will begin to realize the reasons that you are meditating. At that time, mind is nicely composed and happy with very few distractions. There is more peace of mind than has ever been experienced before.

Then, after that experience, you become enthusiastic and want it to happen every time you sit. BUT, that very desire to have those calm states of mind is the very thing which stops them from arising! You then try even harder and put in more effort. Unfortunately, mind only becomes more and more restless and unsettled.

This is due to the desire for something to happen in a particular way. When it doesn't happen that way, you have the tendency to push harder and try to force things to become calm and tranquil.

As a result of your attachment (craving and clinging), your desire to have this occur as you want it to be, you can't experience this calm stage of meditation again. This desire causes you to lean out of the present moment and to try to make the next present moment the way you want it to be. When that present moment isn't right, you try even harder.

However, this calm state of mind will occur again when mind is relaxed and at ease and you don't try to push it. Just relax and let go of that strong desire, calm down and stop expecting things to work according to your own desires and attachments. After the first experience of *Jhāna* (meditation stage of understanding), mind may become quite active the next time you sit in meditation. So, laugh and let it be!

But, now your mindfulness is sharp and is able to recognize when mind's attention goes away quickly. Then you simply let it go, open mind up, relax, smile, and return mind's attention back to the breath and relaxing.

Calming and relaxing on the in-breath, calming and relaxing mind on the out-breath helps the meditation. Before long, mind will settle down again and the joy will arise again. When this joy fades away, you will again experience a tranquil mind that is a very comfortable and happy feeling, as well as a mind that is still and at ease.

At this time, you still have the experience of all the five aggregates (these aggregates are not affected by craving or clinging). You can still hear things, or have feelings arise in the body. For example, you would know when a mosquito or an ant lands on you. You may have some thoughts about that mosquito or ant, but you quickly recognize that this is a distraction, you 6R, and you let it go, relax the tension in the head and mind, smile, then softly come back to the breath and relaxing.

As you continue to relax, open and calm mind on the in and out-breath, eventually you will arrive at a stage where there are no more wandering thoughts and this is when you let go of all of your thinking thoughts. This is commonly called Noble Silence. The joy is a little stronger here, and it lasts a little longer. When it fades away, the comfortable feeling of happiness is stronger and the calm mind goes deeper into the breath and relaxing.

This state is described:
**"again with the stilling of thinking and examining thought, the monk, enters and abides in the second *Jhāna* (meditation stage of understanding), which has self-confidence and singleness of mind without thinking and examining thought, with joy and happiness born of stillness of mind."**

The stilling of thinking and examining thought means that at that time, mind becomes very still and stays on the object of meditation quite nicely. There is no discursive thinking about the past or future. However, there can still be observation thoughts. Remember that true meditation is silent, open observation.

There is still feeling in the body as all of the sense doors are working and the five aggregates are present. But, for example, if a sound arises, it doesn't make mind shake or move. You know where you are and what you are doing.

The self-confidence mentioned in the sutta, comes from the confidence you gain when you see clearly for yourself how well the meditation works. The self-confidence not only arises when you are sitting in meditation but, also during daily activities. The singleness of mind means that mind is very calm and doesn't run around. Mind is very contented to stay on the breath and relaxing and keep opening and relaxing on the in and out-breaths. These are the descriptions of the first two *Jhānas* (meditation stages).

We now return to the Ānāpānasati Sutta.

**He trains thus: 'I shall breathe in experiencing happiness';**
**He trains thus: 'I shall breathe out experiencing happiness.'**

As you continue onwards with your practice and keep calming and relaxing mind, eventually you will reach a stage where the feeling of joy becomes too coarse and it won't arise naturally anymore. This is always a rather comical time for the teacher because the meditator comes to the teacher and says:

Student: 'There's something wrong with my meditation!'
Teacher: 'Why do you say that?'

Student: 'I don't feel any more joy',
Teacher: 'Is that bad?'

Student: 'No, of course not, but still I don't feel any more joy. Why?'
Teacher: 'Do you feel comfortable and more calm than ever before and does your mind have a strong sense of balance in it and you feel very much at ease?'

Student: 'Yes, I feel all of that, but I don't feel any more joy!'
Teacher: 'Good, continue. Everything is going along just fine. Relax and stop demanding that joy arises when you want it to.'

The joy fades away by itself, and a very strong sense of equanimity and calm becomes apparent. You can still hear sounds, and feel contact with the body even though eventually the body seems to disappear. If someone were to touch you during your sitting meditation, you would know it. It someone made a sound, you would hear it but, your mind would not go to it. This is what is meant when the sutta says the meditator has full awareness. It is described as follows:

"Again, with the fading away of joy, a monk abides in equanimity, and mindful and fully aware, still feeling happiness (or pleasure) with the body, he enters upon and abides in the third *Jhāna* (meditation stage), on account of which noble ones announce: 'He has a pleasant abiding who has equanimity and is mindful'.

With the description above, you can plainly see that being in the third *Jhāna* (meditation stage of understanding); mind is very clear, alert and balanced. You are aware of what is happening around you, but mind stays on the object of meditation easily and comfortably.

Being alert (being mindful) and having equanimity in mind is an unusual thing to experience because this state of meditation is the highest and best feeling that you have ever experienced in your whole life. Furthermore, you are not attached to it due to the strong equanimity.

At the same time, both body and mind are exceptionally relaxed and at ease. What a nice state to be in! This is why this state is praised by noble ones. Besides this easing of the tightness in the head, the body looses tension and the feeling of sensations begin to disappear. This is because the tightness in mind causes tension in the body. But now, mind is so comfortable and tension free that the tension in the sensation of the body goes away. When this happens, the body becomes so soft and comfortable that there is nothing to feel. However, you become aware of it if anyone were to touch you. This is the meaning of being mindful and fully aware. Mind knows what is happening around it but it does not shake or become disturbed.

This is what we call experiencing happiness on the in and out-breath.

Some "Fixed Concentration Meditation" teachers say that when one is in this state of *Jhāna*, the meditator can no longer experience the body or any of the sense doors. They claim that the meditator will not know if someone were to hit them with a stick or someone were to change their positions of their hands and feet. This is because their minds are so deeply absorbed into the object that they can't be fully aware. This is clearly not true in the meditation described within the suttas or if one were practicing "Tranquil Wisdom Insight Meditation" (TWIM).

**"He trains thus: 'I shall breathe in experiencing the mental formation';**
**he trains thus: 'I shall breathe out experiencing the mental formation';**
**He trains thus: 'I shall breathe in tranquilizing the mental formation.'**
**He trains thus: 'I shall breathe out tranquilizing the mental formation.'"**

As you continue calming, expanding and relaxing mind, it naturally begins to go deeper. Finally, the feeling of pleasure in the body/mind becomes too coarse and mind experiences exceptional equanimity and balance of mind. It is described thus in the sutta:

"Here with the abandoning of pleasure and pain, and with the previous disappearance of joy and grief a bhikkhu enters upon and abides in the fourth *Jhāna* (meditation stage), which has neither pain or pleasure and purity of mindfulness due to equanimity.'"

When mind's attention becomes very calm and still, you will experience deep tranquility and equanimity of mind. You can still hear sounds and feel sensations with the body, but these things do not shake or move mind at all. Another description of this stage of meditation (*Jhāna*) is:

"My composed mind was purified, bright, unblemished, rid of imperfection, malleable, wieldy, steady and attained to imperturbability."

This gives the serious meditator an idea of what to expect when they attain this stage. Mind's attention is exceptionally clear, bright and alert. Mind can even see when a distraction begins to arise, then let it go and relax, expand mind, and calm down again before smiling and coming back to the breath.

The abandoning of pain and pleasure does not mean that occasionally pain or pleasure won't arise. They will arise, but mind's attention is in such a state of balance that it won't shake or become involved with the distractions. At that time mind is very aware when pain or pleasure arises but the mindfulness and equanimity are so strong that it does not become concerned with it.

With the previous disappearance of joy and grief means your mind's attention has let go of the lower emotional states of liking and disliking. All of the stages of the lower *Jhānas* (meditation states of understanding) involve letting go of emotional states of mind. At first, when you begin to learn about meditation, you let go of very low coarse states which frequently move mind's attention.

After you begin to learn how to calm mind, you can sit for longer periods of time without any distractions arising. You then experience the thinking and examining applications of mind's attention and the other *Jhāna* factors. When mind settles deeper, the thinking and examining of mind disappears. The joy becomes stronger for a while, but gradually it becomes too coarse and mind has too much movement in it.

At that point, mind will naturally go even deeper into the object of meditation and the joy fades away by itself. At this time there is equanimity, happiness, mindfulness and full awareness in mind. All these states of mind are very pleasant experiences.

But eventually, the happiness is too coarse a feeling. So, mind goes deeper into the breath and at the same time, continues opening, expanding, and relaxing. At this point the breath and the relaxing of mind begin to arise together.

Then the happiness fades away and all that remains is strong equanimity, exceptional mindfulness, and composure of mind. This is how one experiences and tranquilizes the mental formations.

As Krishnamurti describes the true meditative state, "A meditative mind is silent. It is not the silence which thoughts can conceive of; it is not the silence of a still evening; it is the silence when thoughts, with all their images, words and perceptions have entirely ceased. This meditative mind is the religious mind—the religion that is not touched by the church, the temples, or by chants."

**20] "He trains thus: 'I shall breathe in experiencing mind'; he trains thus 'I shall breathe out experiencing mind.'"**

At this time, your mind's attention is very calm and any slight disturbance is noticed and is let go of quickly and easily.

First, mind lets go of tightness... now it relaxes and smiles then goes back to the breath and relaxing while expanding and calming on the in-breath and the out-breath.

**"He trains thus: 'I shall breathe in gladdening mind'; he trains thus: 'I shall breathe out gladdening mind.'"**

When you reach this stage of meditation, you begin to experience a finer and more exalted type of joy, which is described as the Joy (*pharaṇapīti*) Awakening Factor.

Mind becomes peacefully happy and at ease like never before. This is called **gladdening mind** because it is such a pleasurable state to be in. At that time, mind is exceptionally uplifted, very clear, and mindfulness is sharper than ever before. The equanimity is even more balanced and composed.

**"He trains thus: 'I shall breathe in stilling mind'; He trains thus: 'I shall breathe out stilling mind.'"**

At this time, mind becomes more subtle and calm, with very few distractions. When they do arise, they are quickly noticed, let go of, relaxed and then you smile and return back to the breath and relaxing.

Naturally, the breath and the relaxing of mind's attention become easier and more serene. They begin to happen together at the same time.

**"He trains thus: 'I shall breathe in liberating mind';
he trains thus: 'I shall breathe out liberating mind.'"**

**Liberating mind** means that you stay on the breath and relaxing
with enough joyful interest so that when mind begins to move
or go away from the breath and relaxing, you are aware of it and
you let the distractions go without any identification. You then
relax mind before smiling and coming back to the breath and
relaxing. When a hindrance arises, you see it quickly and let it go
without hesitation. At this point sloth and torpor, or restlessness
and anxiety, are the biggest obstacles to your practice. Whenever
a hindrance arises, it will knock you out of the *Jhāna* and can
cause all kinds of disturbances.

The phrase **liberating mind** also means to let go of the lower
*Jhānas* (meditation stages of understanding) and all of the *Jhāna*
factors by not being attached (thinking about and identifying
with) them in any way. This is the liberating way of relaxing
craving and experiencing the Third Noble Truth!

**"He trains thus: 'I shall breathe in contemplating
impermanence';
he trains thus: 'I shall breathe out contemplating
impermanence.'"**

As you continue with your practice of meditation on the breath
and relaxing, eventually mind's attention becomes very deep and
then you begin to notice that mind is expanding and getting bigger.
Silence and spaciousness of mind go together. The immensity of
silence is the immensity of mind in which a center does not exist.
Actually, at this time, there is no center and there is no outer
edge. Mind continually grows and expands. You begin to see that
there are no boundaries, and space and mind are infinite.

The Anupada Sutta, sutta number 111 in Majjhima Nikāya, described this as;
**"Again, by passing beyond [gross] perceptions of form, with the disappearance of all [gross] sense of, aware that space is infinite, the monk enters into and abides in the base of infinite space.**

**And the states in the base of infinite space—the perception of the base of infinite space and the unification of mind."**

You still have the five aggregates affected by craving and clinging, contact, feelings, perception, formations, and mind.

**Passing beyond [gross] perceptions of form,** means that even though you know that you have a body at that time, this awareness would not readily pull our mind towards it unless there would be contact at one of the sense doors. In this state of *Jhāna* (meditation stage of understanding), you are very aware of mind's attention and what it is doing.

The disappearance of all sense resistance and non-attraction to the [gross] perceptions of change means, even though a pain arises in the body, you know it but do not get involved with that sensation. You feel mind's attention growing, changing and expanding, but, you are not distracted from the breath or the relaxing of mind. Mind's attention is continually moving and expanding but mind accepts this as it truly is. Seeing impermanence and how mind's attention changes and expands, you realize that this phenomena is part of an impersonal process and you have no control over it. This is a true *anattā* experience.

As you continue on with the practice of opening and returning to the object of meditation, you will eventually start to see individual consciousnesses arising and passing away. It is continually coming up and going away, arising and passing away, without a break! Consciousness keeps coming into being, then vanishing at all the sense doors.

This is described in the Anupada Sutta as:

**"Again, by completely surmounting the base of infinite space, aware that consciousness is infinite, a monk enters upon and abides in 'the realm of infinite consciousness'.**

**And the states in the base of infinite consciousness—the perception of the base of infinite consciousness and the unification of mind."**

You still have the five aggregates, contact, feeling, perception, formations, and mind.

When you are in this state of 'infinite consciousness' and your mindfulness gets weak or distracted, there will arise some hindrances like torpor or dullness of mind, or restlessness. These hindrances arise because the energy that you put into your practice isn't quite correct.

When there is too little energy, you can experience a kind of contraction of mind's attention which is commonly called dullness (rarely does the meditator have sleepiness at this time). On the other hand, if you try too hard or put too much energy into the practice, a distractedness or restlessness will arise. Both of these hindrances will knock you out of the *Jhāna*.

When you are in this state of 'infinite consciousness', you see change happen so rapidly and continually, that it becomes very tiresome. You begin to see just how much un-satisfactoriness (*dukkha*) arises with each consciousness.

Thus, you see up-close and personal, impermanence (*anicca*), suffering (*dukkha*), and you know that you have no control over these events (*anattā*).

You see how these consciousnesses happen by themselves. As a result, you see the not-self or impersonal (*anattā*) nature of this psycho-physical process. This is how you contemplate the 'Three characteristics of all existence' (*anicca, dukkha, anattā*). It is not done by thinking about it but by realizing it through your own personal experience.

We return now to the Ānāpānasati Sutta.

**"He trains thus: 'I shall breathe in contemplating fading away'; he trains thus: 'I shall breathe out contemplating fading away.'"**

As you continue on with your practice on the in-breath, letting go and relaxing mind, and on the out-breath, letting go and relaxing mind, mind naturally lets go of all consciousnesses which were so readily seen before. Mind then gets into the "realm of nothingness". This is when there is no external thing for mind to see. Mind is not looking at anything outside of itself at this time.

The Anupada Sutta says this:

**"Again, by completely surmounting the base of infinite consciousness, aware that there is 'nothing'; the Bhikkhu enters upon and abides in the base of nothingness.**

**And the states in the base of 'nothingness'—the perception of the base of nothingness and the unification of mind, again there are still the five aggregates, contact, feeling, perception, formations, and mind."**

As odd as this may sound, it is an exceptionally interesting state to be in. There are still many things to watch and observe although there is nothing to see outside of mind and mental factors. You still have the five aggregates, and some of the hindrances will still pop-up whenever you become either too lax or too energetic.

It is here that the "Seven Awakening Factors" become very important. They can be seen one by one as they occur. When torpor arises, you must put mind's attention back into balance by arousing the "Awakening Factor of Mindfulness" (*Sati*), the "Awakening Factor of Investigation of your experience" (*Dhammaviyama*), the "Awakening Factor of Energy" (viriya), and the "Awakening Factor of Joy" (*pharaṇapīti*). This is the way to overcome the hindrance of torpor.

If restlessness arises, you must bring up the feeling of the "Awakening Factor of Mindfulness" (*Sati*), the "Awakening Factor of Tranquility (passadhi), the "Awakening Factor of Collectedness" (*samādhi*), and the "Awakening Factor of Equanimity" (*upekkhā*). (More will be discussed later.) This is the way to overcome the hindrance of restlessness.

At this time, mind becomes very stricky. It becomes very interesting to see the subtle ways it distracts you from your meditation object. However, your mindfulness is quite strong and these tricks can be seen very easily and they can be 6Red very easily.

Back to the Ānāpānasati Sutta:

**"He trains thus: 'I shall breathe in observing cessation';
he trains thus: 'I shall breathe out observing cessation.'"**

You still continue on relaxing mind on the in and out-breath. At this time, mind's attention begins to get smaller and it seems to shrink. Mind becomes very subtle and still. This is described in the Anupada Sutta as:

*"Again, by completely surmounting the base of nothingness, the monk enters upon and abides in the base of 'neither-perception nor non-perception (which is also neither feeling nor non-feeling, and neither consciousness nor non-consciousness)"*.

Mind's attention becomes so subtle and small, and has such little movement or vibration in it, that it is sometimes difficult to know whether there is mind's attention or not. It is also difficult to know if there is perception for mind. This extremely fine state of mind is not easy to attain. Yet, it is attainable if you continue on with the instructions given by the Buddha of staying with the 6R's.

At this time, you cannot see the breath any longer, but there are still some things that can arise. This state is like being in the state of sleep but being aware at the same time. At first, it will only last for a few minutes. When you come out of that state, you have to reflect on what happened while you were in that state. Some of the things you can remember are shapes, colors, or forms. As soon as you remember anything, you must 6R it immediately.

This is when you begin to sit for long periods of time. The meditation is the total tranquilizing and releasing of all energy. This is where you are purifying your mind at its finest. Also you become unconscious of time. The longer you sit in this exquisite peacefulness, the better. You might begin to sit for three, four or five hours and this can be extended during retreats or at home if you have the time.

At this time, you can still experience an occasional subtle vibration of mind's attention. As you continue on with your practice and keep opening, relaxing and calming your mind, in a very subtle way, mind becomes very fine and it does not move at all. Eventually you will experience the state called "the Cessation of Perception, Feeling and Consciousness" (nirodha-samapatti).

**"He trains thus: 'I shall breathe in observing relinquishment'; he trains thus: 'I shall breathe out observing relinquishment.'"**

This state of meditation is not the experience of the Supramundane *Nibbāna* yet. But, it is very close to that time. When you come out of the cessation of perception, feeling, and consciousness, you will next see very clearly the arising of all of the links of Dependent Origination. That is because when formations arise, then consciousness arises; when consciousness arises, then mentality/materiality arises; when mentality/materiality arises, then 6 sense doors arise; when the 6 sense doors arise, then contact arises; when contact arises, then feeling arises; when feeling arises, then craving arises; when craving arises, then clinging arises; when clinging arises, then habitual tendency arises; when habitual tendency arises, then birth arises; when birth arises, then ageing and death, sorrow, lamentation, pain grief and despair arise. This is the arising of this whole mass of suffering.

Then you will see that when formations do not arise, then consciousness doesn't arise; and so on and when ignorance does not arise, there are no more conditions and that is the cessation of all of this whole mass of suffering.

You will experience the Supramundane *Nibbāna* when you see all of this arising and passing away and you will understand so deeply that the big "OH WOW!" of *Nibbāna* occurs. This happens after the perception, feeling, and consciousness comes back and is noticed.

Upon observing the final letting go of all conditioned things, there is a huge shift in your mind. It becomes dispassionate, and completely lets go of the belief in a permanent unchanging self or soul.

This is the only way you will experience the supramundane state of *Nibbāna*, that is, by seeing directly all of the links of Dependent Origination through the eyes of the Four Noble Truths and the Three Characteristics of all Existence.

This is why it is called the 'Doctrine of Awakening'. The Anupada Sutta description is as follows:

*"Again, by completely surmounting the base of neither-perception nor non-perception, the monk enters upon and abides in the cessation of perception, feeling and consciousness. And his taints are destroyed by his seeing with wisdom."*

When you are in the state of the "Cessation of Perception, Feeling, and Consciousness, you will not know that you are in that state. Why? It is because you do not have any perception, feeling, or consciousness at all!

It is like all the lights were turned off on a very dark night. At that time you can not see anything at all, not even if you were to put your hands in front of your face.

Now, you may sit in this state for a period of time. When the perception, feeling and consciousness comes back, and if your mindfulness is sharp enough, you will see directly all of the Links of Dependent Origination, and the Four Noble Truths quickly and automatically.

It does not matter whether you have studied the links of

Dependent Origination or not. This is direct knowledge, not memorized or studied knowledge.

The statement: **'And his taints are destroyed by his seeing with wisdom'** means seeing and realizing all of the links of Dependent Origination and the Four Noble Truths directly.

It was said many times in the texts that, *"One who sees Dependent Origination sees the Dhamma and one who sees the Dhamma sees Dependent Origination."* But in order to see the origin of suffering you have to know what suffering is! Thus, if you see the ceasing of the suffering i.e., the Third Noble Truth, you will naturally see the Fourth Noble Truth.

You must practice the way leading to the cessation of the suffering in order to see the other three Noble Truths. And this is the Fourth Noble Truth. Thus, seeing Dependent Origination directly means that you see and realize all of the Four Noble Truths. This is how you observe relinquishment.

Back to the Ānāpānasati Sutta:

**22] "Monks, that is how mindfulness of breathing is developed and cultivated so that it is of great fruit and great benefit"**

**Fulfillment of the Four Foundations of Mindfulness**

**(Observation of Body) [Kāyanupassana]**
**23] "And how, monks, does mindfulness of breathing, developed and cultivated, fulfill the Four Foundations of Mindfulness?**

**24] "Monks, on whatever occasion a monk, breathing in long, understands: 'I breathe in long,' or breathing out long understands: 'I breathe out long'; Breathing in short, understands: 'I breathe in short,' or breathing out short, understands: 'I breathe out short'."**

The phrase 'on whatever occasion', is very interesting and has far reaching implications. 'On whatever occasion' does not mean only while sitting in meditation, but, all of the time.

During your daily activities, when mind becomes heavy and full of thoughts, as you notice it, simply let go of the thoughts, calm and relax the tightness in your head, feel mind expand and become tranquil and then smile and go back to the breath, relax and smile for one or two breaths. This will help you greatly in calming mind and it will improve your mindfulness during your daily activities.

The more you smile during your daily activities, the better your mindfulness becomes. This is definitely a practical way to practice your daily activities and improve your awareness of states of consciousness. Every time you do this during your daily activities, it brings a kind of awareness and perspective into your life. It becomes easier to see the three characteristics of existence of impermanence, suffering, and the impersonal nature of everything, even while you are working or playing.

The statement, 'On whatever occasion', extends into your Walking Meditation as well. Instead of putting mind's attention onto your feet, (as some meditation teachers recommend), you can still keep your attention on observing mind, and relaxing on the in and out-breath, while walking. This is mindfulness of body and can even extend into other activities.

Mindfulness of mind objects is a very important aspect to be aware of and is much easier to watch than the physical body. It is easy to tell when mind is tight and tense. If you only have a little time, you can release the mental hold of whatever you are thinking about, relax the tightness in the head, then smile, and come back to the breath and relaxing for one or two breaths.

Remember that the first and second verses in the Dhammapada, *"Mind is the forerunner of all (wholesome and unwholesome) states. Mind is chief; mind made are they."*

Everything follows mind, be it happiness or suffering. By trying to follow all the movements of the body, you cannot see mind clearly enough to realize the tightness caused by that movement.

Becoming aware of mind and all of its movements and tendencies to tighten was what the Buddha intended, when he said **"On any occasion"**.

**He trains thus: 'I shall breathe in experiencing the whole body';
He trains thus: 'I shall breathe out experiencing the whole body:
He trains thus: 'I shall breathe in tranquilizing the bodily formation';
He trains thus: 'I shall breathe out tranquilizing the bodily formation'—**

**On that occasion a monk abides observing the body as a body, ardent, fully aware, and mindful, having put away covetousness and grief for the world. I say that this is a certain body among the bodies, namely, in-breathing and out-breathing. That is why on that occasion a monk abides observing the body as a body, ardent, fully aware, and mindful, having put away covetousness and grief for the world.**

The statements about experiencing the whole body, and the tranquilizing of the bodily formation has already been discussed. Thus, we won't repeat that section here.

**Observing the body as a body** is self-explanatory about the breath. Being **'ardent'** means 'working hard', or 'being ever alert'. **Fully aware and mindful,** is pertains to the alertness of mind when it is in the *Jhānas* (meditation stages of understanding) as well as during daily activities.

When you are in the "Tranquil Wisdom Insight *Jhānas*", you are definitely very aware of what is happening around you and your mindfulness is sharp and clear. You are able to observe all mind states, feelings, sensations, or distractions as well as the *Jhāna* factors when they arise in mind, i.e., joy, happiness, equanimity, stillness of mind, calm composure of mind etc.

**Having put away covetousness and grief for the world,** means mind has gone beyond the simple liking and disliking of distractions, emotions, painful feeling, pleasant feeling, happy feeling, and the thinking about them. It means to let go of attachment to things (craving and clinging) which cause suffering to arise.

The rest of the paragraph is just repeating that the breath meditation is part of mindfulness of breathing, and that it conforms with the First Foundation of Mindfulness of the Body.

**25] "Monks, on whatever occasion,**
**a monk trains thus: 'I shall breathe in experiencing joy';**
**He trains thus "I shall breathe out experiencing joy;**
**He trains thus "I shall breathe in experiencing happiness';**
. **He trains thus: 'I shall breathe out experiencing happiness';**
**He trains thus: 'I shall breathe in experiencing the mental**

formation';
he trains thus: 'I shall breathe out experiencing the mental formation';
He trains thus: 'I shall breathe in tranquilizing the mental formation';
He trains thus: 'I shall breathe out tranquilizing the mental formation'—

This is again a repetition of the previous section, and thus, we shall continue without further delay.

### (Observation of Feeling) [*Vedanānupassana*]

"On that occasion a monk abides observing feeling as feeling, ardent, fully aware, and mindful, having put away covetousness and grief for the world. I say that this is a certain feeling among feelings, namely, giving close attention to the in-breathing and out-breathing.

That is why on that occasion a monk abides observing feeling as feeling, ardent, fully aware, and mindful, having put away covetousness and grief for the world."

This is from the Satipaṭṭhāna Sutta and further explains about how the meditator becomes more alert through mindfulness of feeling:

#32] "*And how, monks, does a monk abide observing feeling as feeling? Here, when feeling a pleasant feeling, when a monk feels a painful feeling, a monk understands 'I feel a pleasant feeling': when feeling a neither pleasant nor painful feeling, he understands: " I feel a neither pleasant nor painful feeling.' When feeling a worldly pleasant feeling, he understands; 'I feel a worldly pleasant feeling' When feeling an unworldly feeling, he understands: 'I feel an unworldly feeling pleasant feeling'; when feeling a painful worldly feeling, he understands: 'I feel a painful worldly feeling'; when feeling a painful unworldly feeling, he understands: 'I feel a painful unworldly feeling'; when feeling a neither pleasant nor painful worldly feeling, he understands: 'I feel a worldly neither pleasant nor painful feeling'; When feeling an unworldly neither pleasant nor painful feeling, he understands: 'I feel an unworldly neither pleasant nor painful feeling.'*

*A worldly feeling* describes whatever feeling that arises at any of the senses doors (that is the eye, ear, nose, tongue, body or mind). An *unworldly pleasant feeling* is when a meditator is in any of the four *Jhānas* (which includes all of the *arūpa* or immaterial *Jhānas*). When you are experiencing a worldly painful feeling this means that you are experiencing a painful feeling at one of the sense doors. For example when you stub your toe a painful worldly feeling arises.

*An unworldly painful* is a meditation pain. You can identify a meditation pain because when you get up and walk, the pain goes away. However, a real physical pain does not go away when you get up to walk. It is important to change your position for sitting if physical pains arise so that you do not hurt your body.

When you feel *a neither pleasant-nor-painful worldly feeling,* this is a neutral feeling that you have indifference to and the tendency to ignore and this leads you to not being mindful at that time.

*An unworldly neither pleasant-nor-painful feeling* is when you are in any of the *Jhānas* and experience equanimity.

This describes all kinds of feeling (i.e. pleasant, painful, or neither pleasant-nor-painful feeling). This is how you get to experience the different stages of meditation. If you stop being attentive to the breath and relaxing, your meditation progress stops as well. The importance of staying with the breath and relaxing cannot be understated. This is how the "Second Foundation of Mindfulness of the Feeling" is fulfilled.

**26] "Monks, on whatever occasion a monk trains thus: 'I shall breathe in experiencing mind';**
**He trains thus: 'I shall breathe out experiencing mind';**
**He trains thus: 'I shall breathe in gladdening mind';**
**He trains thus: 'I shall breathe out gladdening mind';**
**He trains thus: 'I shall breathe in stilling mind';**
**He trains thus: 'I shall breathe out stilling mind';**
**He trains thus: 'I shall breathe in liberating mind';**
**He trains -thus: 'I shall breathe out liberating mind'."—**

Again this next part is from the Satipaṭṭhāna Sutta and discusses many aspects of the *Jhānas*.

**(Observation of Mind) [*Cittānupassana*]**

**#34]** *"And how, monks, does a monk abide observing mind as mind? Here a monk understands mind affected by lust as mind affected by lust, and mind unaffected by lust as mind unaffected by lust. He understands mind affected by hate as mind affected by hate. He understands mind unaffected by hate as mind unaffected by hate. He understands mind affected by delusion as mind affected by delusion and mind unaffected by delusion as mind unaffected by delusion.*

*A mind affected by lust, hate, and delusion* actually means a mind affected by craving. Craving is the "I like it" (lust mind) or the "I don't like it" (hatred mind) and delusion is taking whatever arises as being ours personally (this is "ME"). So, lust,, hatred and delusion are always referring to the craving mind.

*He understands contracted mind as contracted mind,*

A contracted mind is a mind that has sloth and torpor in it,

*And distracted mind as distracted mind.*

A distracted mind is a mind that has restlessness or anxiety in it.

*He understands exalted mind as exalted mind, and unexalted mind as unexalted mind.*

An exalted mind is a mind that experiences one of the *rūpa* or material *Jhānas.*

*He understands surpassed mind as surpassed mind, and unsurpassed mind as unsurpassed mind.*

A surpassed mind is a mind that can get into any of the *arūpa* or immaterial realms—that is the realm of infinite space, the realm of infinite consciousness, the realm of nothingness, and the realm of neither perception nor non-perception.

*He understands, collected mind as collected mind and uncollected mind as uncollected mind. He understands, liberated mind as liberated mind, and unliberated mind as unliberated mind.*

These last two sentences are pretty much self explanatory.

*"On that occasion a monk abides observing mind as mind, ardent, fully aware, and mindful, having put away covetousness and grief for the world. I do not say that there is development of mindfulness of breathing and relaxing for one who is forgetful,*

*who is not fully aware. That is why on that occasion a monk abides observing mind as mind, ardent, fully aware, and mindful, having put away covetousness and grief for the world."*

The statement, *"I do not say there is development of mindfulness of breathing and relaxing for one who is forgetful, who is not fully aware"* is one of the strongest statements made in the Satipaṭṭhāna Sutta. The function of mindfulness is to remember.

To remember what? To remember to observe how mind's attention moves from one thing to another, then relax the tightness caused by that movement and to always come back to the meditation object with joyful interest, and clear comprehension.

When you are in the "Tranquil Wisdom Insight *Jhānas"* (meditation stages of understanding) your mind becomes extraordinarily clear, bright, and alert. As you go deeper and deeper along the path, more profound states of mind present themselves. Mindfulness and full awareness becomes so refined that even the slightest movement of mind's attention can be observed and 6Red, let go of and relaxed into. Mind becomes clear, more expanded, and spacious, free from tension, and the breath and relaxing becomes clearer and easier to watch.

Your mind's attention begins to be unwavering and mind develops more composure than ever before. This particular part of the foundations of mindfulness describes how to notice when mind is experiencing each of the stages of *Jhāna* from the material *Jhānas* (*Rūpa Jhānas*) all the way up and through the immaterial *Jhānas* (*Arūpa Jhānas*). This is how the "Third Foundation of Mindfulness of Mind" is fulfilled.

**27] "Monks, on whatever occasion a monk trains thus: 'I shall breathe in observing impermanence and relaxing';**

He trains thus: 'I shall breathe out observing impermanence and relaxing';
He trains thus: 'I shall breathe in observing fading away and relaxing';
He trains thus: 'I shall breathe out observing fading away and relaxing';
He trains thus: 'I shall breathe in observing cessation';
He trains thus: 'I shall breathe out observing cessation';
He trains thus: 'I shall breathe in observing relinquishment';
He trains thus: 'I shall breathe out observing relinquishment'"—

This, is referring to the immaterial *Jhānas* (*Arūpa Jhānas*, or meditation stages of understanding) again and how you experience the attainment of the Supramundane *Nibbāna*.

This sutta teaches you how to reach all of the meditation stages and to attain the highest bliss through the seeing and understanding of all the links of Dependent Origination and the Four Noble Truths, through the fulfillment of the "Four Foundations of Mindfulness", and the balancing of the Seven Awakening Factors.

Now, again we will go the Satipaṭṭhāna Sutta which talks about the Fourth Foundation of Mindfulness. This particular section has five different parts and explains how the entire foundation actually works.

**(Observation of Mind Objects) [*Dhammanupassana*]**

**1. The Five Hindrances**

*#36] "And how, monks, does a monk abide observing mind-objects as mind-objects? Here a monk abides observing mind-*

*objects as mind-objects in terms of the five hindrances. And how does a monk abide observing mind-objects as mind objects in terms of the five hindrances? Here there being sensual desire in him, a monk understands 'there is sensual desire in me'; or there being no sensual desire in him a monk knows 'there is no sensual desire in me', and he also understands how there comes to be the arising of the unarisen sensual desire, and how there comes to be the abandoning of the arisen sensual desire, and how there comes to be the future non-arising of the abandoned sensual desire.'"*

You understand that your mindfulness has faded away and the unarisen sensual desire of this hindrance has arisen. So, when your mindfulness becomes weak and disappears, then this hindrances will arise. This happens because you have lost keen interest in your meditation object.

*How there comes to be the abandoning of the hindrance of sensual desire* is by remembering to use the 6R's. That is, **recognizing** that mind is distracted, **releasing** or letting go and not keeping your attention on that hindrance, **relaxing** the tightness in your head caused by that distraction, **re-smiling** to bring up a wholesome object, **returning** to your meditation object, and to **repeating this same cycle if needed while** using your meditation object for as long as possible—this is the 6R's.

*How there comes to be the future non-arising of the hindrance.* This happens by taking a strong interest in your meditation object which may be the breath or Loving-kindness depending on your choice of meditation.

## 2. The Five Aggregates

*#38] "Again, monks, a monk abides observing mind-objects as*

*mind-objects in terms of the Five Aggregates affected by craving and clinging."*

There are many different ways to translate about the five aggregates—one translator translates it as the 'clinging aggregates' which is very misleading because it implies that the aggregates always have clinging attached to them. This is not always true. Another translator calls it the 'five aggregates affected by clinging'. Again, this may be misleading because it places too much emphasis on just the clinging and doesn't give the cause of the clinging.

When the author gives a Dhamma talk sometimes when he comes across the aggregates he says 'the aggregates may or may not be affected by craving and clinging' depending on one's mindfulness at the time. Of course this is a little awkward to put in a book. So, it is used the way it is above. The words craving and clinging need to be mentioned with the five aggregates because this seems to be the best way to remind the meditator that this is a part of a process and is linked to the direct knowledge and experience of Dependent Origination.

Satipaṭṭhāna Sutta:
#38] *Here a monk understands 'Such is material form, such its origin, such its disappearance; such is feeling, such its origination, such its disappearance; such is perception, such its origin, such its disappearance; such are thoughts (formations), such their origin, such their disappearance; such is consciousness, such its origin, such its disappearance.*

Ānāpānasati Sutta:
#39] **On that occasion a monk abides observing mind-objects as mind-objects, ardent, fully aware, and mindful, having put away covetousness and grief for the world. Having seen with wisdom the abandoning of covetousness and grief, he closely**

looks on with equanimity. That is why on that occasion a monk abides obsserving mind-objects as mind-objects, ardent, fully aware, and mindful, having put away covetousness and grief for the world.

When you experience the higher *Jhānas* (meditation stages of understanding), your mind develops a finer and finer balance in it.

You then experience the 'abandoning of covetousness and grief, he closely looks on with equanimity'. You see clearly how tricky mind truly is, and you keep a sense of equanimity in it, even though some unpleasant things may arise. The true balance of meditation is learned when you go into the immaterial realms of mind. This is when there is a real letting go of mental concepts and attachments. Mind develops such a beautiful equanimity that even when the most unpleasant feeling arises, mind will accept it without being disturbed. This is how the Fourth Foundation of Mindfulness of Mind-Objects is fulfilled.

Ānāpānasati Sutta:
28] "Bhikkhus, that is how Mindfulness of Breathing, developed and cultivated, fulfills the Four Foundations of Mindfulness."

## Fulfillment of the Seven Awakening Factors

29] "And how, monks, do the Four Foundations of Mindfulness, developed and cultivated, fulfill the Seven Awakening Factors?"

30] "Monks, on whatever occasion a monk abides observing the body as a body, ardent, fully aware, and mindful, having put away covetousness and grief for the world—on that occasion unremitting mindfulness is established in him. On whatever occasion unremitting mindfulness is established in a monk—on that occasion the Mindfulness Awakening Factor is aroused in him, and he develops it, and by development, it comes to fulfillment in him."

Let us use a description from the Satipaṭṭhāna Sutta for more clarification. It says:

#42] "Here, there being "Mindfulness Awakening Factor" in him, a monk understands: 'There is "Mindfulness Awakening Factor" in me'; or there being no "Mindfulness Awakening Factor" in him, he understands: 'There is no "Mindfulness Awakening Factor" in me'; and he also understands how there comes to be the arising of the unarisen "Mindfulness Awakening Factor" and how the arisen "Mindfulness Awakening Factor" comes to fulfillment by development.

This is rather straight forward. It simply says that you know when your mind is silent, sharp, clear, and joyfully interested in the breath and relaxing and the other things which arise. You also know when mindfulness is dull, not sharp, and mind's attention tends to be a little bored or disinterested.

When that happens, you know that you must pick-up your interest and see how everything that arises is truly different.

You then see how every breath and relaxing is different. It is never exactly the same.

This is how the arisen "Mindfulness Awakening Factor" comes to fulfillment by development.

Ānāpānasati Sutta:
31] **Abiding thus mindful, he investigates and examines that state with wisdom and embarks upon a full inquiry into it. On whatever occasion, abiding thus mindful, a monk investigates and examines that experience with wisdom and embarks upon a full inquiry into it—on that occasion the "Investigation-of-Experience Awakening Factor" is aroused in him, and he develops it, and by development it comes to fulfillment in him.**

It is very important to be familiar with the "Factor of Investigation-of- your-Experience". This means whatever arises, whether it is any of the five hindrances, an emotional state, or a physical feeling, you impersonally examine how this arose. We are not interested in why it arose! The "why" is for psychologists.

For Buddhists, "how" the process actually works is the most important thing to observe and seeing it with interest is very important. This is done by not getting involved with thinking about that phenomenon, but only observing it's presence, allowing it to be there, then 6R-ing it—letting it go mentally— by opening up that tight mental fist which has grabbed onto it, relaxing, expanding and allowing that distraction to be there by itself without keeping your attention on it; then, relaxing the tightness in mind/head, smiling and redirecting mind's attention back to the breath and relaxing.

Every time mind is pulled away, you see the different aspects about that distraction. Then let it go, relax mind, smile and come back to the breath and relaxing. In this way, you become more familiar with HOW the distraction arises and are able to recognize it more quickly. This type of investigation is described in the Satipaṭṭhāna Sutta as:

*#42] "Here, there being the "Investigation-of-Experience Awakening Factor" in him, a monk understands: 'There is the "Investigation-of- Experience Awakening Factor" in me'; or there being no "Investigation-of-Experience Awakening Factor" in him, he understands: 'There is no 'Investigation-of-Experience Awakening Factor" in me'; and he also understands how there comes to be the arising of the unarisen "Investigation-of-Experience Awakening Factor"; and how the arisen "Investigation-of-Experience Awakening Factor" comes to fulfillment by development.*

To bring forth the "Awakening Factor of Investigation-of-Experience", you have to take a strong interest in how everything works.

In other words, you have to discover what happens first, what happens next, what happens after that? The more you examine your experience, the easier it is to recognize all of the different and unusual aspects about the hindrances and distractions. When you see these things clearly, it is much easier to let go of them and to relax into them. It is also important to develop the perspective that this is an impersonal (*anattā*) process which is unsatisfactory (*dukkha*) and is always changing (*anicca*). This perspective enables you to progress without periods of confusion.

Ānāpānasati Sutta:
**32] "In one who investigates and examines that state with wisdom (seeing how Dependent Origination works) and embarks upon a full inquiry into it, tireless energy is aroused. On whatever occasion tireless energy is aroused in a monk who investigates and examines that state with wisdom and embarks upon a full inquiry into it—on that occasion the energy enlightenment factor is aroused in him, and he develops it, and by development it comes to fulfillment in him.**

It takes a lot of energy and effort when one takes sincere interest into what is happening in the present moment and examines it with care. As you use your energy and have a strong joyful interest, this causes even more energy to arise.

This is described in the Satipaṭṭhāna Sutta as:
#42] *"Here, there being the energy enlightenment factor in him, a monk understands: 'There is the energy enlightenment factor in me'; or there being no energy enlightenment factor in him, he understands: 'There is no energy enlightenment factor in me'; and he also understands how there comes to be the arising of the unarisen energy enlightenment factor and how the arisen energy enlightenment factor comes to fulfillment by development.*

Ānāpānasati Sutta:
**33] "In one who has aroused energy, unworldly joy arises. On whatever occasion unworldly joy arises in a monk who has aroused energy—on that occasion the Joy Awakening Factor is aroused in him.**

(Unworldly joy (*pharaṇapīti*) refers to all pervading joy.

On whatever occasion unworldly joy arises in a Bhikkhu who has aroused energy—on that occasion the joy enlightenment factor is aroused in him, and he develops it, and by development it comes to fulfillment in him.

As one has more energy in staying on the breath, their mindfulness becomes sharper and their energy increases little by little. When this happens, mind becomes quite happy and delights in staying on the breath and expanding mind. This happy feeling is a type of feeling without so much excitement and is very nice and cooling to mind.

These states of mind are not to be feared or pushed away. It is a natural process when one develops and progresses along with their practice of meditation to experience these states. If they stay on the breath and open their minds with interest and do not get involved with the joy, no problems will arise.

The Satipaṭṭhāna Sutta says:

*#42] "Here, there being the joy enlightenment factor a Monk understands: 'There is the joy enlightenment factor in me; or there being no joy enlightenment factor in him, he understands: 'There is no joy enlightenment factor in me'; and he also understands how there comes to be the arising of the unarisen joy enlightenment factor, and how the arisen joy enlightenment factor comes to fulfillment by development.*

These first four enlightenment factors are very important when one experiences sloth and torpor. Sloth means sleepiness, and torpor means dullness of mind. When one gets into the fourth *Jhāna* and above, the two main hindrances which arise are restlessness and, sloth and torpor.

However, when one brings up the investigation factor of enlightenment and examines this torpor, they have to use more energy and this helps to overcome the dullness. When you get into the higher *Jhānas* you must learn to fine tune their practice little by little. By being familiar with these enlightenment factors, you will learn how to eventually balance all of the factors. This directly leads to the supramundane state of *Nibbāna*.

The most important key for success in meditation is the first enlightenment factor of mindfulness. Without mindfulness, one cannot possibly reach any of these meditation stages. Mindfulness is the main key to overcome both sloth and torpor, and restlessness.

Remember these hindrances can come at any time and knock the meditator right out of any of the meditation stages, even up to the realm of neither-perception nor non-perception. Thus, you must be very careful to recognize these enlightenment factors and be skillful in learning how to use them when it is appropriate. The next three enlightenment factors are important to overcome restlessness.

Ānāpānasati Sutta:
**34] "In one who is joyful, the body and mind become tranquil. On whatever occasion the body and mind become tranquil in a Monk who is joyful—on that occasion the tranquility enlightenment factor is aroused in him, and he develops it, and by development it comes to fulfillment in him.**

When joy arises in mind, one feels very pleasant feelings in the body and mind. This is true, even in the higher stages of meditation, like the immaterial states of *Jhāna* (meditation stages). After awhile, the joy fades a little and one's mind becomes exceptionally calm and peaceful. This state is called the enlightenment factor of tranquility. At that time, one's body and mind become extraordinarily peaceful and calm.

The Satipaṭṭhāna Sutta describes it thus:
*#42 "Here, there being the tranquility enlightenment factor in him, a Monk understands: 'There is the tranquility enlightenment factor in me'; or there being no tranquility enlightenment factor in him, he understands, 'There is no tranquility enlightenment factor in me'; and he also understands how there comes to be the arising of the unarisen tranquility enlightenment factor and how the arisen tranquility enlightenment factor comes to fulfillment by development.*

Actually, the strongest part of the tranquility enlightenment factor is the mental feeling which is very nice, calm and with a feeling of strong peace. This is especially noticed when one is experiencing the first three immaterial *Jhānas* (meditation stages) which are the realm of infinite space, the realm of infinite consciousness and the realm of nothingness.

Ānāpānasati Sutta:

**35] "In one whose body is tranquil and who feels pleasure, mind becomes still and composed. On whatever occasion mind becomes still and composed in a Monk whose body is tranquil and who feels pleasure—on that occasion the stillness enlightenment factor is aroused in him, and he develops it, and by development it comes to fulfillment in him.**

(This is frequently called the concentration enlightenment factor, but this term is too misunderstood. So the author prefers to use stillness enlightenment factor)

As your mind and body become more tranquil and at ease, mind stays on the breath and relaxing and mind expands more naturally, without any distractions. It is much easier to open and relax mind with each in and out-breath. Mind is definitely composed and unruffled by any external or internal distractions. There comes a time when mind prefers to stay still on the meditation object, without undue force or trying to concentrate. It stays on the breath for very long periods of time. Of course, at this time, there is very sharp mindfulness and full awareness.

You still has full awareness even when they reach the realm of nothingness. Mind does not waver or move away from the breath even though one hears sounds or knows that a mosquito has landed on them.

Mindfulness of breathing and stillness are very clear and sharp to observe. When you is in the realm of nothingness, you can explore and watch many different aspects of mind.

Their mind is also very clear, even though one is in the lower meditation stages. Since mind is still, you can observe things quite clearly, too. This can be called the action of silence. When mind is absolutely silent, it is the blessing that everyone is seeking.

The Satipaṭṭhāna Sutta describes this as:
#42] *"Here, there being the stillness enlightenment factor in him, a Monk understands: 'There is the stillness enlightenment factor in me'; or there being no stillness enlightenment factor in him, he understands: 'There is no stillness enlightenment factor in me'; and he also understands how there comes to be the arising of the unarisen stillness enlightenment factor and how the arisen enlightenment factor comes to fulfillment by development."*

Ānāpānasati Sutta:
36] **"He closely looks on with equanimity at mind thus stilled and composed. On whatever occasion a Monk closely looks on with equanimity at mind thus stilled and composed—on that occasion the equanimity enlightenment factor is aroused in him, and he develops it, and by development it comes to fulfillment in him."**

The equanimity enlightenment factor is again, a very important factor to develop. It balances mind when it becomes unsettled. The equanimity enlightenment factor is the only factor which allows mind to lovingly-accept whatever arises in the present moment. For example, if there arise any kinds of pain (physical or emotional), it doesn't disturb mind's attention.

The equanimity enlightenment factor is the factor which helps you to see things impersonally and without the ego-identification of getting involved with distractions. It is the seeing of what arises in the moment, then going beyond it with balance. The seeing of *anattā* (impersonal nature of everything) is the very thing which allows you to progress rapidly along the Buddha's Path. But you must be somewhat careful with equanimity because it is often mistaken to be indifference. Indifference has some dissatisfaction and aversion in it, but not equanimity. Equanimity has sharp mindfulness in it; dissatisfaction has no mindfulness in it.

Equanimity has only openness and complete acceptance of everything that arises in the present moment. It is the complete impersonal perspective. Equanimity opens mind totally. Indifference closes it, and tries to ignore what is happening in the moment.

The Satipaṭṭhāna Sutta describes it thus:
#42] *"Here, there being the equanimity enlightenment factor in him, a Monk understands: 'There is the equanimity enlightenment factor in me'; or there being no equanimity enlightenment factor in him, he understands: 'There is no equanimity enlightenment factor in me'; and he also understands how there comes to be the unarisen equanimity enlightenment factor and how the arisen equanimity enlightenment factor comes to fulfillment by development."*

These last three enlightenment factors, tranquility, stillness, and equanimity factors, will greatly assist you when restlessness arises in mind. Restlessness makes mind think many thoughts and causes lots of unpleasant feelings to arise in the body. As a result, you feel like breaking your meditation and distracting yourself in one way or another. To say the least, it is a noticeable hard tight mind that causes suffering.

The only way to overcome restlessness is by developing stillness of mind and tranquility of body. When mind has restlessness in it, there is no balance of mind at all. Instead, there is a lot of ego identification with that feeling. Thus, to overcome this hindrance, you have to allow it to be there by itself and relax. By bringing forth the stillness, tranquility, and equanimity enlightenment factors and focusing mind on these different factors, you will overcome the restlessness.

The two major hindrances that always seem to trouble meditators are torpor, dullness of mind, and restlessness.

You had better become friends with these two hindrances, because they will stay around until you become an *Arahat*. The sooner we drop all resistance to these states when they arise and begin to explore them with joyful interest, the faster we will be able to recognize them. As a result, we will be able to let them go faster and return into the *Jhāna* (meditation stage).

Ānāpānasati Sutta:
**37] Monks, on whatever occasion a Monk abides contemplating feeling as feeling, ardent, fully aware, and mindful, having put away covetousness and grief for the world...**
(this whole formula repeats itself again starting at section 30 and continuing on until section number 36)
**the equanimity enlightenment factor is aroused in him, and he develops it, and by development it comes to fulfillment in him."**

Please realize that you must use these enlightenment factors whenever any hindrance or distraction arises. It does not matter if the hindrance arises during your sitting meditation or during your daily activities. These factors put mind in balance whenever it gets bumped by a distraction.

And so, this goes on through all of the Four Foundations of Mindfulness. It shows you how to use the seven enlightenment factors at all times while practicing mindfulness of Breathing Meditation. These enlightenment factors do arise one by one as they occur and not all at the same time. Also, it shows the importance of *Jhānas* (meditation stages) for the development of mind and how there is great fruit and great benefit to be enjoyed when you follow these simple instructions.

38] "Monks, on whatever occasion a Monk observes mind as mind, ardent, fully aware, and mindful, having put away covetousness and grief for the world...
(Again, this repeats from section 30 to section 36)
the equanimity enlightenment factor is aroused in him, and he develops it, and by development it comes to fulfillment in him."

39] "Monks, whatever occasion a Monk abides observing mind-objects as mind-objects, ardent, fully aware, and mindful, having put away covetousness and grief for the world...
(repeat section 30 to 36)
the equanimity enlightenment factor is aroused in him, and he develops it, and by development it comes to fulfillment in him."

40] "Monks, that is how the Four Foundations of Mindfulness, developed and cultivated, fulfill the Seven Enlightenment Factors."

When the Seven Awakening Factors are in perfect balance, the possibility of attaining the Supramundane *Nibbāna* occurs. As you go higher and higher in the *Jhānas* (meditation stages), the balance of the enlightenment factors becomes finer and much more subtle. This fine tuning of mind becomes so interesting that you want to naturally sit for much longer periods of time. This meditation is by far the best show in town!

Some meditators get up very early in the morning so that they have enough time to watch and learn the balance of mind and still go to work. This meditation turns out to be the most gratifying and fun exploration that you could ever experience, during any of your activities.

### Fulfillment of True Knowledge and Deliverance

41] **"And how, Monks, do the Seven Enlightenment Factors, developed and cultivated, fulfill true knowledge and deliverance?**

42] **"Here, Monks, a Monk develops mindfulness enlightenment factor, which is supported by seclusion, dispassion, and cessation, and ripens in relinquishment.**

The term **"supported by seclusion"** means that one must gain the lowest *Jhāna* (meditation stage). As was stated above, the description of the first *Jhāna* starts with **"to be secluded from sensual pleasure, then to be secluded from unwholesome states"**. At that time, mind is alert and stays on the object of meditation with clarity, i.e. no distractions.

If a distraction begins to arise, mindfulness recognizes that and lets it go. Next, the description says the happiness experienced comes about by being born of seclusion. This is how the mindfulness enlightenment factor is supported by seclusion.

Dispassion means mind is free from attachments and clinging, i.e., not thinking or analyzing. Gaining to the fourth *Jhāna* (meditation stage) means to reach a stage of having an imperturbable mind, or a mind that has such strong equanimity that it becomes dispassionate. This is how the mindfulness enlightenment factor is supported by dispassion.

Cessation here means the ceasing of defilements and ego-identification with what arises.

Being mindful is a term that always had a kind of slippery meaning and it is not what most people think. Its meaning is very simple and precise when it is seen as observing mind, or attention, or alertness of attention. Being truly mindful means to see what mind is doing at all times, then let go of the things that cause tension to arise in the head, relax and tranquilize both body and mind. It includes observing how this whole process works and allows it to be, without getting involved in the drama of things. Not getting involved with the drama of things means, to not identify with, or take personally this impersonal process or try to control the present moment.

'Being mindful' means 'to lovingly open one's mind and let go of all identification with that distraction, then relax the tension in the head and in mind', so that one can see things clearly and calmly. Whenever you try to resist or control what is happening in the present moment, at that time, you are fighting with the 'Dhamma' or 'Truth of the Present Moment'.

This fighting with the reality of the present moment causes so much un-satisfactoriness and suffering to arise. However, when you are mindful and see clearly that this is just phenomena arising and passing away, you can open up and accept it, without hardening your mind or resisting in any way. This time, joyful interest is very important because when mind has some joy in it there is no anger, jealousy, aversion, fear, or anxiety, etc.

Joyful interest helps the meditator to have the proper perspective to impersonally see what happens in the moment. When mind is uplifted, you see that whatever arises is just part of a continuing process which you can learn from. Joy causes mind to be uplifted, which is why it is an enlightenment factor and very important to one's practice. Also, when joy is in your mind, you are pleasant to be around.

Remember, the acronym that is very helpful to use is **DROPSS**. It stands for Don't Resist Or Push, SMILE and Soften mind and accept everything when it occurs, because that is the 'Dhamma of the Moment'.

When you continue on with your practice, mind will eventually attain to the higher and more subtle stages of meditations (*Arūpa Jhānas*). At that time, mind experiences the realm of 'nothingness'. This is what is called cessation. It is called this because there is nothing more to watch outside of mind. When you experience the realm of 'nothingness', mind is watching nothing. But mind is still there and the different enlightenment factors can arise along with the five aggregates which are affected by clinging.

Also, some hindrances can still arise and knock you out of that exalted state. Thus, there is nothing for mind to watch outside of itself, and yet, there is still lots to see. This is how the mindfulness enlightenment factor is supported by cessation.

When you experience the realm of neither-perception nor non-perception, and keep opening and relaxing mind, eventually you will experience the cessation of perception and feeling (*Nirodha-Samāpatti*). During this occurrence, you will not know this turning off of consciousness because you have no perception or feeling at all! This is the only stage of meditation where this phenomenon occurs. This meditation state is still mundane; it is not the Supramundane *Nibbāna* yet.

How can you know what is happening without perception or feeling? It is only when the perception and feeling come back, and if mindfulness is sharp enough, will you can see directly, each and every link of Dependent Origination forwards, one by one as they occur. Even this is not the Supramundane State of *Nibbāna*.

The links are:
When ignorance arises, then formations arise;
when formations arise, then consciousness arises;
when consciousness arises, mentality-materiality arises;
when mentality-materiality arises, then the six-fold sense base arises;
when the six-fold sense base arises, contact arises;
when contact arises, feeling arises;
when feeling arises, craving arises;
when craving arises, then clinging arises;
when clinging arises, then habitual tendencies arise;
when habitual tendencies arise, birth arises;
when birth arises, then old age, death arises.

After this arising phenomenon ends, and at that point, you will experience the cessation of the Dependent Origination, which goes like this:

When ignorance ceases, formations will not arise;
when formations cease, consciousness will not arise;
when consciousness ceases, mentality/materiality will not arise
when the six-fold sense base ceases, contact will not arise;
when contact ceases, feeling will not arise;
when feeling ceases, craving will not arise;
when craving ceases, then clinging will not arise;

when clinging ceases, then habitual tendencies will not arise;
when habitual tendencies cease, birth will not arise;
when birth ceases, old age and death, sorrow lamentation, pain,
grief, and despair, cease.
That is the end of the whole mass of suffering.

The seeing of Dependent Origination both forwards and in
reverse order leads mind to the attainment of the 'Supramundane
*Nibbāna*'.

This is where there is a major change in your outlook. Your
mind at that time becomes dispassionate about the belief in
a permanent everlasting ego or self. You see from first hand
experiential knowledge, that this is just an impersonal process
and there is no one controlling the way phenomena arise. They
arise because conditions are right for them to arise. In Buddhist
terms, this is called *'anattā'* or not-self nature of existence.

You also realize that no one can possibly attain sainthood by
the practice of mere chanting words or phrases or suttas, or the
practice of having rites and rituals done for you by someone else
or by yourself. You have no more doubt about what is the correct
path that leads to the higher stages of purity of mind towards
Arahatship. This is how you become a *Sotāpanna* and attain the
true path of purification.

There is no other way to attain these exalted stages of being. It
is only through the realization of the Noble Truths by seeing
Dependent Origination. Merely seeing the three characteristics
will not now, nor ever be the experience which leads to the
'Supramundane *Nibbāna*'.

This is why all of the Buddha's appear in the world, to show the
way to realizing the Four Noble Truths.

He develops the mindfulness enlightenment factor....
The investigation of experience enlightenment factor ...
the energy enlightenment factor...
the joy enlightenment factor...
the tranquility enlightenment factor...
the stillness enlightenment factor...
the equanimity enlightenment factor,
which is supported by seclusion, disenchantment, dispassion,
and cessation, which ripens in relinquishment.

Ānāpānasati Sutta:
**43] "Monks, that is how the Seven Enlightenment Factors,
developed and cultivated, fulfill true knowledge and
deliverance."**

Since this sutta describes the Four Foundations of Mindfulness
and the Seven Enlightenment Factors, the author will conclude
with the last part of the Satipaṭṭhāna Sutta. This is taken from
the Majjhima Nikāya sutta number 10, sections 46 to 47. It says:

*46) "Monks, if anyone should develop these Four Foundations
of Mindfulness in such a way for seven years, one of two fruits
could be expected for him: either final knowledge here and now,
or if there is a trace of clinging left, non-return."*

This means attaining to the state of being an *Anāgāmī* or non-
returner

*"Let alone seven years, Monks. If anyone should develop these
four foundations of mindfulness in such a way for six years... for
five years... for four years... for three years... for two years... for
one year, one of two fruits could be expected for him: either final
knowledge here and now, or if there is a trace of clinging left,
non-return."*

*"Let alone one year, Monks. If anyone should develop these Four Foundations of Mindfulness in such a way for seven months... for six months... for five months... for four months... for three months... for two months... for one month... for a half month ..., one of two fruits could be expected for him: either final knowledge here and now, or if there is a trace of clinging left, non-return."*

*"Let alone half a month, Monks. If anyone should develop these Four Foundations of Mindfulness in such a way for seven days, one of two fruits could be expected for him: either final knowledge here and now, or if there is a trace of clinging left, non-return."*

*47) "So, it was with reference to this that it was said: 'Monks, this is a 'direct path' ...*
Some translations say **'This is the only way'**, but that doesn't say it in the correct way—**a direct path or way**, says this much more clearly and with less confusion.
*... for the purification of beings, for the surmounting of sorrow and lamentation, for the disappearance of pain and grief, for the attainment of the true way, for the realization of Nibbāna— namely, the Four Foundations of Mindfulness.'*

*That is what the Blessed One said. The Monks were satisfied and delighted in the Blessed One's words."*

This is a pretty big claim which is not made up by the author. He is only reporting what is in the suttas. When you are serious about the practice of developing mind through the 'Tranquility' of the 'Mindfulness of Breathing', you can reach the final goal.

When you reach the first pleasant abiding (the first *Jhāna*) and if you continue on with their practice, you have the potential to attain either the stage of *'Anāgāmī'* or *'Arahat'*. This is what the Buddha said. If you are ardent, and continues without changing or stopping in your practice, then surely you will reach the goal which is described.

Again, remember that the only way to attain the Supramundane *Nibbāna* is by realizing Dependent Origination both forwards and in reverse order. There is no other way because this is the seeing and realizing of the Four Noble Truths which forms the main teaching of the Buddha. Great fruits and benefits accrue to those who practice according to the instructions prescribed by the Buddha.

SĀDHU... SĀDHU... SĀDHU....

If there are any mistakes in this book, the author takes full responsibility and requests that these mistakes be pointed out to him. The sincere wish of the author is that all who practice meditation, will continue on with their efforts until they reach the highest and best state possible, that is, the attainment of Final Liberation, the Supramundane *Nibbāna*.

May all those who are sincere, know and understand the Four Noble Truths and Dependent Origination through direct knowledge, attain the highest goal. May all practitioners of the Buddha's path, realize all of the links of Dependent Origination quickly, and easily in this very lifetime; so that their suffering will soon be overcome.

* * * * * * *

The author would like to share the merit accrued by the writing of this book with his parents, relatives, helpers and all beings so that they can eventually attain the highest Bliss and be free from all suffering

## Sharing of Merit

May suffering ones be suffering free
And the fear struck fearless be.
May the grieving shed all grief
And may all beings find relief.
May all beings share in this merit
That we have thus acquired
For the acquisition of
all kind of happiness.
May beings inhabiting space and earth
Devas and Nagas of mighty power
Share in this merit of ours.
May they long protect
the Buddha's Dispensation.
Sādhu! Sādhu! Sādhu!

---

**Footnotes**

[1] The author refers to the Ānāpānasati Sutta, which includes the Four Foundations of Mindfulness, as well as the Seven Enlightenment Factors.
[2] See Thus Have I Heard. The Long Discourses of the Buddha, translated by Maurice Walshe, Wisdom Publications (1987), p.556.
[3] See Mahāsaccaka Sutta, sutta number 36 of Majjhima Nikāya.
[4] This means all nine of them! They are the four material *Jhānas*, the four immaterial *Jhānas* and the cessation of perception and feelings.
[5] Here, the word *'Jhāna'* carries the meaning of absorption concentration (*appanā samādhi*), or access concentration (*upacāra samādhi*)— This is the stage right before mind becomes absorbed

into the object of meditation. These are the standard definitions as given by other teachers.

[6] In this context, it only means absorption (*appanā samādhi*) and not access concentration (*upacāra samādhi*).

[7] Some meditation teachers call this momentary concentration or moment-to-moment concentration (*khanika samādhi*)

[8] Notice the plural form of the word sutta—this means seeing the agreement many times.

[9] This ceremony marks the end of the rains retreat where the Bhikkhus gathered together to confess any slight wrong doing which they may have committed.

[10] This refers to talking and idle gossip. The Bhikkhus waited patiently, and quietly doing their own meditation practices of expanding the silent mind and having clear mindfulness while waiting for the Buddha to speak.

[11] This refers to mindfulness of the body, mindfulness of feelings, mindfulness of consciousness, and mindfulness of mind objects.

[12] For example, see Mahāsakuludayi Sutta, sutta number 77 and Anupada Sutta, sutta number 111. Both of these suttas are found in the Majjhima Nikāya.

# 2
# Loving-kindness
# Meditation

One of the favorite things I like to do with students who have ever practiced the breath meditation without the 6R's, is to ask them to take *Mettā* as their object of meditation while they learning TWIM first. I do this because it is easier for them to progress without having to break old bad habits from a previous practice, before they can learn to 6R smoothly.

IF they are not progressing extremely well, later on, they can decide to go back to the breath. But usually students do not because of how much emphasis the Buddha placed on practicing this meditation in the texts. The Loving-kindness Meditation was practiced far more often then the Breathing Meditation. When bad habits are already operating with breath mediation it makes is very hard to investigate a new practice. If their cup is full they have to empty it before they can taste something new. If you can learn Loving-kindness from an empty cup, you are in great shape with a beginner's mind.

So, right up front, I am going to suggest that you try TWIM in this way and let the breath or any other practice go for awhile; at least for two weeks to a month to see what can happen. When you practice, please follow the instructions VERY carefully and exactly.

Now, these instructions were given by me on July 3, 2000, at the Washington Buddhist Vihāra in Washington, DC and to this day, they have not changed much at all. They include the practice of "Tranquil Wisdom Insight Meditation" (TWIM) and the practice of the "Four Foundations of Mindfulness" at the same time.

These instructions may be a little different than what you are used to, because this I have followed the instructions given in the suttas very closely. If you practice in this way, the end results can bring great benefit to you and all other people around you. This, in turn, will bring true happiness in your daily life.

## Loving-kindness Meditation

When practicing Loving-kindness Meditation, you first start by sending loving and kind thoughts to yourself. Begin by remembering a time when you were happy. When the feeling of happiness arises, it is a warm glowing or radiating feeling in the center of your chest. Now, when this feeling arises, make a very sincere wish for your own happiness and feel that wish. "May I be happy"... "May I be filled with joy"... "May I be peaceful and calm"... "May I be cheerful and kind", etc.

Make any wholesome sincere wish that has meaning for you, feel the wish in your heart, and radiate that smiling feeling. The key word here is "**sincere**". If your wish isn't a sincere wish, then it will turn into a mantra, that is, it may become a statement repeated by rote, with no real meaning. Then you would be on the surface repeating the statement while thinking about other things. So, it's really important that the wish you make for yourself, and later for your spiritual friend, has real meaning for you and uses your whole undivided attention. You then feel that wish and put that smiling feeling into your heart and radiate it.

Don't continually repeat the wish for happiness: "May I be happy... may I be happy... may I be happy... may I be happy". Make the wish for your own happiness and feel that wish when the feeling of Loving-kindness begins to fade a little.

## Relax Tension

The following step is a very important part of the meditation:

After every wish for your own happiness, please notice that there is some slight tension or tightness in your head, in your mind. Let it go. You do this by relaxing mind completely then smiling. Feel mind open up and become calm, but, do this only one time.

If the tightness doesn't go away, never mind, you will be able to let it go while on the meditation object (your home base).

Don't continually try to keep relaxing mind without coming back to the home base. Always softly redirect your smiling tranquil attention back to the radiating of happiness.

One problem that many meditators seem to have is that they try too hard! This meditation needs to be done with a soft relaxed mind, not pushing or making mind stay on the Loving-kindness. If you try too hard then it will cause you to have a headache. So please do this Loving-kindness lightly, have fun with meditation, and smile a lot. The more you smile, the easier the meditation becomes, and your mindfulness will improve by leaps and bounds.

**How to Sit**

When you sit in meditation please do not move your body at all. Sit with your back nicely straight, but not rigid. Try to have every vertebrae stacked comfortably one on top of the other. This position has the tendency to bring your chest up a little, so it can be easier to radiate the feeling of love and the wish.

Sit with your legs in a comfortable position. If you cross them too tightly, the circulation in your legs may stop, causing your legs to go to sleep and this becomes very painful. If you need to sit on a cushion or even in a chair, that is okay. If you sit in a chair, however, please don't heavily lean back into it. Leaning heavily back stops the energy flow up your back and can make you feel sleepy. Just sit in a comfortable way.

The most important part of this is to sit completely still. Please don't move your body at all while sitting. Don't wiggle your toes; don't wiggle your fingers; don't scratch; don't rub; don't rock your body; don't change your posture at all. In fact, if you can sit as still as a Buddha image, this would be the best! If you move around, it becomes a big distraction to your practice and you won't progress very quickly at all.

While you are sitting, radiating the warm—glowing feeling of Loving-kindness in the center of your chest, making and feeling the sincere wish, and feeling that wish in your heart, your mind will wander away and begin to think about other things. This is normal.

## Arising Thoughts

Thoughts are never your enemy! So, please don't fight with them or try to push them away or try to suppress them. When a series of thoughts come up to take you away from your meditation object, notice that you are not smiling or experiencing the feeling of Loving-kindness and making a wish for your own happiness. Then, simply let go of the thought. This means to let the thought be there by itself without keeping your attention on it. Even if you are in mid-sentence, just let go of the thought, don't keep your attention on it, let it be there by itself. This is done by not continuing to think the thought, no matter how important it seems at that time.

At this point there is another very important step:

## Notice Tension

Notice the tightness or tension in your head/mind, now relax. There are two halves to everyone's brain. There is a membrane called the "meninges" surrounding these two halves. Every time a thought, feeling, or sensation arises this membrane tightens around the brain.

This tightness is how craving (*taṇhā*) can be recognized and let go of. This is also called the cause of suffering or the "Second Noble Truth". Relaxing this tightness is the way of letting go of craving which is called the cessation of suffering or the "Third Noble Truth"! Feel the tightness open. The brain (a part of the body) and mind feels like it expands and relaxes. It then becomes very tranquil and calm.

At this time there are no thoughts and mind is exceptionally clear, alert, and pure because now there is no more craving or clinging. Immediately smile and then bring that soft smiling mind back to your object of meditation, that is, the feeling of Loving-kindness and making and feeling the wish for your own happiness.

It doesn't matter how many times your mind goes away and thinks about other things. What really matters is that you see "HOW" your mind has become distracted by a thought. The same method holds true even for any sensation or emotional feeling that pulls your attention to it. In that case just notice "HOW" the movement of mind's attention occurs, "HOW" mind becomes distracted, and let that distraction go.

Now, relax the tightness or tension in your head/mind, softly smile and redirect your calm attention back to the object of meditation.

**Strengthen Awareness**

Learn to let go of any distraction, make a wish for your happiness, and then relax the tightness caused by the movement of mind's attention, and redirect your smiling tranquil attention back to the feeling of being happy. Every time you return to the Loving-kindness and make that wish and smile, you are strengthening your mindfulness (observation power). Please, don't criticize yourself because you think that you "should" do better, or that your thoughts, feeling, sensations and emotional feelings are the enemy to be squashed and destroyed.

These kinds of critical hard-hearted thoughts and feelings contain aversion, and aversion is the opposite of the practice of "Loving-Acceptance". Loving-kindness and Loving-Acceptance are different words that say basically the same thing. So please be kind to yourself. Make this a fun kind of game to play with, not an enemy to fight with.

The importance of relaxing the tightness or tension after every thought, sensation, or emotional feeling can't be stated enough. When you let go of this tightness you are letting go of craving. It is very important to understand this because craving is the cause of all suffering. This tightness or tension is where our wrong idea about ego-identification occurs. This is how the personal perspective (wrong view) arises.

**Craving and Ego-Identification**

Craving and the false idea of a personal "self" ("I", "Me", "Mine") always manifests as tightness or tension in your head/mind. When you let go of tightness, what you are actually doing is letting go of craving and the false idea of a personal "self". You are letting go of "ego-identification" with all of the thoughts, bodily feelings, sensations, and emotional feelings, opinions, concepts, etc. that arise. This is referred to as clinging (*upādāna*). When you let go of this tightness in mind (craving) you don't have clinging arise, which means that all these thoughts, opinions, concepts, ideas, and stories about why you like or dislike things won't arise to disturb mind and pull your attention away from relaxing and having fun with your meditation. This is how you purify your mind and become happier and more uplifted, all of the time!

While you are sitting still, there may be some sensations that arise in your body. You may feel an itch, heat, tension, a feeling of coughing or wanting to sneeze, or pain. **Please don't move your body at all**. When such a feeling arises, your mind will immediately go to that feeling, let's say an itch or cough.     You don't have to direct mind, it goes by itself. The first thing mind does is think about the feeling: "I wish this would go away."... "I want this to stop bothering me."... "I hate this feeling."... "Why doesn't it just go away?"... "I want this to stop."

Every time you entertain these kinds of thought, the sensation becomes bigger and more intense. It actually turns into an emergency in your mind. Then you won't be able to stand it anymore, and you have to move. **But the instructions are: don't move your body for any reason at all.** Watch the movements of mind's attention instead.

So what can you do? You need to open up and allow the feeling to be there, without trying to change it or make it go away:

**Opening Up**

First, notice that your mind's attention has gone to the itch or cough, etc., and the thoughts about that sensation. Now, let go of those thoughts, simply let them be there without keeping your attention on them. Next notice the tightness in your head/mind and relax.

Every time a sensation (or emotional feeling) arises, it is only natural for mind to wrap a mental tight fist around it; this tight mental fist is aversion.     So, open up and allow the itch (or emotional feeling) to be there. Remember that it is okay if the tightness doesn't go away immediately.

The "Truth (Dhamma) of the present moment", is that when an

itch or any other sensation arises, **it is there**. What you do with this Dhamma dictates whether you will suffer more unnecessarily or not. Resisting the itch and trying to think it away, trying to make it different than it is, produces more both subtle and gross pain.

**Five Aggregates**

We have five different things or bunches of things that make up this mind/body process, they are called the Five Aggregates.

They are:
1. Physical Body (*kāya*)
2. Feeling (*vedanā*)
3. Perception (*saññā*)
4. Thought (formations—*saṅkhara*)
5. Consciousness (*viññāṇa*)

As you can see feelings, are one thing and thoughts (formations) are another. If you try to control your feelings with your thoughts, the resistance that you have to this feeling causes it to get bigger and more intense. In fact, it becomes so big that it turns into a true emergency (real un-satisfactoriness—*dukkha*), and you can't stand the sensation (or emotional feeling) anymore. Then you have to move. While you are sitting in meditation, if you move your body even a little bit, it breaks the continuity of practice and you have to start over again.

Letting go of the thoughts about the sensation (or emotional feeling) means that you are letting them be there by themselves without keeping your attention on them. The want to control the feeling with your thoughts is only natural, but, it leads to immeasurable amounts of suffering! It also means that you are letting go of craving when you relax, which directly leads to the cessation of suffering.

Next, you notice the tight mental fist wrapped around the sensation, and, let go of that aversion to it. Simply allow the itch or cough (sensation or emotional feeling) to be there by itself. See it as if it were a bubble floating in the air and let the bubble float freely. Whichever way the wind blows, the bubble will float in that direction. If the wind changes and blows in another direction, the bubble goes in that direction without any resistance at all.

This practice is learning how to lovingly-accept whatever arises in the present moment. Now, again notice that subtle tightness or tension in your head/mind, relax, smile, and softly redirect your gentle loving attention back to the feeling of radiating love from your heart and making a wish for your own happiness.

**The 6R's:**

The true nature of these kinds of feeling (which includes both mental and emotional feelings), and sensations are that they don't go away right away. So, your mind will bounce back and forth from your object of meditation and to that feeling (that is smiling, radiating the feeling of love, and then making and feeling a sincere wish for your happiness). Every time this happens you use the 6R's which are:

**\*Recognize – \*Release – \*Relax – \*Re-smile – \*Return – \*Repeat**

The 6R's is the way to remember this practice:

**Recognize**: Be alert or mindful with what arises in the present moment. Recognize any distractions that pull mind's attention from the meditation object.

**Release**: Let go of any thoughts, sensations or emotional feelings. Remember its O.K. for that thought, sensation, or emotional feeling to be there because that is the truth (Dhamma) of the present moment. Allow the thought, sensation, or emotional feeling to be, without trying to make it be anything other than it is.

**Relax**: Relax the tightness! Let go of the tight mental fist around the feeling and let it be. Tranquilize both body and mind.

**Re-Smile**: Remember that this is a smiling meditation and it is helpful to smile as much as possible.

**Return**: Come back to your object of meditation by gently re-directing your tranquil attention back to radiating the feeling of love, making a sincere wish for your happiness, and feeling that wish in your heart.

**Repeat**: Continue on with your meditation of radiating Loving-kindness, making and feeling the wish, and visualizing your spiritual friend for as long as you can.


**Radiating Love to a Spiritual Friend**

After sending loving and kind thoughts to yourself for about ten minutes, then begin sending loving and kind thoughts to your "spiritual friend". A "spiritual friend" is someone who, when you think of them and their good qualities, it makes you happy.

This is a friend who is of the same sex, they are alive, and not a member of your family. This is for right now. Later, you will be able to send Loving-kindness to all of the members of your family. But for this training period please choose a friend that you love and respect.

Once you start sending Loving-kindness to your spiritual friend, please don't change to another person. Stay with the same spiritual friend until you get to the third meditation stage (*Jhāna*). As you are sending a sincere wish for your own happiness and then, mentally you say, "As I wish this feeling of peace and calm (happiness, joy, whatever) for myself, I wish this feeling for you, too. May you be well, happy and peaceful." Then start radiating this feeling of love and peace to your friend. It is quite important for you to feel the sincere wish and that you place that feeling in your heart.

**Visualization**

You also visualize your friend in your mind's eye. For example, you can visualize your friend as if they are in a photograph or you can see them moving around as if in a movie. For some people visualizing can be somewhat difficult because they don't realize that one can visualize with words as well as pictures in their mind. Saying your friends name and using some words that help to see that person in your mind's eye is fine! The exact visualization doesn't matter. But when you see your friend, see him or her smiling and happy. This can help to remind you to be smiling and happy too!

The visualization can be somewhat difficult. It can be cloudy, or fuzzy, or a long distance away. It can be there for just a moment and disappear. That's all right. Don't try too hard because it will give you a headache. You want about 75% of your attention spent on the feeling of Loving-kindness, 20% (more or less, depending on what is happening) on making a sincere wish and feeling that wish in your heart. This helps the feeling for your friend's happiness to grow. Only about 5% of your time should be spent on visualizing your friend. As you can see, the *Feeling of Loving-kindness* is by far the most important part of the meditation, and the visualization is the least important part. But still put a little effort into the visualization. Eventually, it will get better and easier.

## Smiling

This is a smiling meditation. While you are sitting and radiating love to your spiritual friend or to yourself, smile with your mind. Even though your eyes are closed during the meditation, smile with your eyes. This helps to let go of tension in your face. Put a little smile on your lips and put a smile in your heart. Smiling is nice and most helpful to practice all of the time, but especially when you are sitting in meditation. The more we can learn to smile the happier mind becomes.

It may sound a little hokie, but scientists have discovered that the corners of our mouth are very important. The position of the lips corresponds to different mental states. When the corners of your lips turn down, your thoughts tend to become heavy and unwholesome. When the corners of your lips go up, mind becomes more uplifted and clear so that joy can arise more often.

This is important to remember because a smile can help you to change your perspective about all kinds of feelings and thoughts. So try to remember to smile into everything that arises and everything that you direct your mind's attention to. In other words, smile as much as you can into everything.

## Dullness of Mind

The more sincere and enthusiastic you are in sending Loving-kindness to yourself and your spiritual friend, the less you will experience sleepiness or dullness of mind. When sleepiness or dullness occurs, your body may begin to slump. This is the only time that you can move your body to straighten up. But don't do this too often, either.

If you see your mind starting to dull out, then take more interest in your friend; see him or her doing things that you truly appreciate. For example, you can visualize times that they were helpful and generous, or times when they made you happy and you laughed with them. This can help to increase your interest and energy, and then the dullness will subside.

Please, once you begin this meditation, start by sitting for 30 minutes. The first ten minutes you send Loving-kindness to yourself. The rest of the time, send love to your spiritual friend (remember to use the same friend all of the time). When your meditation becomes better and you feel more comfortable, you can sit for a longer periods of time (whatever is appropriate for you with your time constraints). But, don't sit for less than 30 minutes a day in the beginning! Sit more if you have the time.

**Active Meditation**

This is not simply a passive meditation to be practiced only when you are sitting in a chair or on a cushion. It's a meditation to be practiced all of the time, especially when you do your daily activities. So many times we walk around in a mental haze of random nonsense thoughts. Why not try practicing Loving-kindness Meditation whenever we can possibly remember? When you are walking from your house to your car, or your car to your job, what is your mind doing? Ho-humming probably about more nonsense thoughts.

This is the time to notice what your mind is doing in the present moment and to let go of these distracting thoughts. Relax the tightness in your head/mind and wish someone happiness! It doesn't matter who you send loving thoughts and feelings to in your daily activities. It can be to the person walking next to you, your spiritual friend, yourself, or all beings. The key words here are to "send love", smile, and feel that sincere wish. Try to do this as much as possible during the day. The more we focus on sending and radiating loving and kind thoughts, the more we affect the world around us in a positive way. As a result, your mind becomes uplifted and happy. Nice!

**Benefits of Loving-kindness**

There are many benefits to practicing Loving-kindness:
1.   You sleep peacefully.
2.   You wake up peacefully, easily, and mind is very alert.
3.   Disturbing dreams do not occur.
4.   People like you.
5.   Animals like you.
6.   You are protected by the Devas
7.   You are not affected by misfortune from, fire, poison, and weapons.
8.   Meditation progress is faster with this meditation than any other meditation.
9.   Your face becomes radiant and beautiful.
10.  You die with a mind free from confusion.
11.  If the stage of sainthood if not reached during this lifetime, one will be born in a Brahmā world.

When you practice Loving-kindness, your mind goes deeper in meditation and more quickly than with any other type of meditation.

Actually, the Buddha mentioned Loving-kindness Meditation well over 100 times and he taught the "Mindfulness of Breathing" meditation only 8 times in the suttas. So, you can see just how important he thought it was.

**Loving-kindness and *Nibbāna***

The practice of Loving-kindness Insight Meditation can lead you directly to the experience of *Nibbāna* if you follow all of the *Brahmā Vihāras* precisely. The *Brahmā Vihāras* include the practice of Loving-kindness, Compassion, Joy, and Equanimity. This is mentioned many times in the suttas which are the original discourses of the Buddha.

Many times other teachers will say that this practice alone doesn't directly lead the meditator to the experience of *Nibbāna*. But, when Loving-kindness Insight Meditation is practiced as part of the *Brahmā Vihāras* (the heavenly abodes), it will take the meditator "automatically", without changing the meditation instructions, to the material (*Rūpa Jhānas*) and immaterial realms (*Arūpa Jhānas*) up to the realm of nothingness. All of the *Brahmā Vihāras* actually arise by themselves.

This opens the path for you to experience the realm of "neither perception nor non-perception" and "the cessation of perception, feeling, and consciousness" which happens right before you see and truly understand how the impersonal links of Dependent Origination and the Four Noble Truths occur. When this is seen and fully understood it is such an eye-opening experience that *Nibbāna* takes place.

There is a very special sutta called "The Simile of the Saw" (sutta number 21, Majjhima Nikāya) which shows the usefulness of practicing Loving-kindness in your daily life. In order to attain *Nibbāna* you must decide to change old unwholesome habits of acting and speaking into the wholesome habits of having equanimity and Loving-kindness towards everyone you see or think about. This sutta shows how to practice your meditation during your daily activities and this simple instruction leads to true happiness all of the time.

It says:

*"There are these five courses of speech that others may use when they address you: Their speech may be timely or untimely, true or untrue, gentle or harsh, connected with good or with harm, spoken with a mind of loving-kindness or with inner hate. When others address you their speech may be timely or untimely; when others address you their speech may be true or untrue; when others address*

*you their speech may be gentle or harsh; when others address you their speech may be connected with good or with harm; when others address you their speech may be connected with loving-kindness or with inner hate."*

*"You should train thus: "My mind will remain unaffected, and I shall utter no evil words; I shall abide compassionate for their welfare, with a mind of loving-kindness, without inner hate. I shall abide pervading that person with a mind imbued with loving-kindness; and starting with them, I shall abide pervading loving-kindness to the all-encompassing world with a mind that is abundant, exalted, immeasurable, without hostility and without ill-will."*

*"If you keep this practice in mind, do you see any course of speech, trivial, or gross, that you could not endure? Therefore, you should keep this advice in mind always and that will lead to your welfare and happiness for a long time."*

This is a good reason to remember to smile all of the time. There are many advantages to smiling and one of the main reasons is because smiling will show you what true mindfulness is. Another reason is when you smile a lot, joy arises very easily while you are doing your daily activities. When joy arises, mind is exceptionally bright, clear, alert, and agile. It is easy to see when mind starts to get pulled down into unwholesome states and with that mindfulness present it becomes very easy to 6R and come back to smiling.

I hope these instructions are helpful and that by practicing in this way you will benefit greatly and lead a truly happy and healthy life.

# 3
# Forgiveness Meditation

A great tool for life's little toolbox!

Forgiveness Meditation can be a useful tool. It is a part of Loving-kindness Meditation. It can help open the heart and mind if there seems to be any blockage in the beginning of your practice.

Forgiveness Meditation can be used when someone dies and there seems to be a great overwhelming grief. It helps relieve depression very much and can rebalance a person. Any accompanying suffering that might follow any catastrophic event can be helped by forgiveness work

One thing about Loving-kindness Meditation is that you cannot give what you do not have. We spend more time with ourselves then anyone else while we are alive and sometimes we need to forgive and love ourselves before we can give anything to others. Forgiveness can help with many other memories from the past that you might be attached and which can be blocking your progress in the Loving-kindness Meditation.

Therefore, the Forgiveness Meditation is a way of opening yourself up to the possibilities of true healing so that you can send love to yourself and to others. This is a soft gentle way of learning how to lovingly-accept whatever arises and to leave it be, without trying to control it with thoughts.

Sometimes in our lives there can be a feeling of letting someone down by not doing enough to help them. Of course, this is just mind saying "I should've been better; I could've done better; I would've done better; I failed and I am not worthy and because of that I should suffer even more".

Forgiveness Meditation is not ever to be used as a club to beat away a feeling of sadness, anger, frustration, or any other kind of feeling. Once again, the Forgiveness Meditation is a soft gentle way of learning how to lovingly-accept whatever arises and to leave it be, without trying to control it with your thoughts.

Of course, these unwholesome blaming kinds of thoughts and feelings don't have anything to do with reality. We don't need to blame ourselves for our friends or a family member's decision to take their own life, to die, or to dive into depression, anxiety, or anger. It is always a difficult situation to have to cope with such circumstances and there are a few things that you can do for yourself and others around you in the case of a death or suicide. This can help the deceased person as well.

**Forgiveness Meditation Instructions**

This meditation is done by sitting down and beginning the process of forgiveness by forgiving yourself for:

1] not understanding,
2] for making mistakes,
3] for causing pain to myself or anyone else,
4] for not acting the way I should have acted.

The way you do this practice is by first forgiving yourself. This is done by taking each of these four statements, one at a time, such as "I forgive myself for not understanding" and saying it over and over again.

You then place that feeling of forgiveness in your heart and radiate that feeling of soft acceptance to yourself.

The thing is, mind is tricky and you will sometimes have huge resistance to forgiving yourself. You will come up with all kinds of thoughts to distract or blame yourself. But when you see mind taking off and thinking unwholesome things, then gently 6R those thoughts and feelings, while gently redirecting your attention back to forgiving yourself again.

Sit with that feeling of loving-acceptance for as long as it lasts. Then, make the statement again to help the loving-acceptance last even longer.

Mind will naturally have a lot of "yes, but... yes, but... yes, but..." interruptions and try to distract you and condemn you and make you feel guilty or sad or angry or whatever it wants to do.

This is where patience needs to be cultivated. Softly allow those distracting (hindrances) to be there and then gently bring your attention back to forgiving yourself. Do this softly with the 6R's practice cycle.

Of course your mind will naturally go to the person who died or committed suicide. When that happens then softly, gently, start forgiving them for 1] not understanding, or 2] making mistakes, or 3] for causing pain and suffering to themselves and to you, or 4] for not acting in the way they should have acted. Forgive them for everything.

See them in your mind's eye and look into their eyes and forgive them. Keep repeating one of these statements (whichever one that seems most appropriate at the time), or you can make up your own statement of forgiveness if it seems right.

It is best not to get involved with a story with that person in your own mind. It is best to forgive them by using the same statement over and over again. "I forgive you for _____."

Then, place that forgiveness into your heart with the person who died and stay with that feeling or forgiveness for as long as it lasts. At first this may not be for very long, to be sure, so, whenever mind becomes distracted, softly, gently, 6R that distraction and start over again.

After a period of time (during that sitting), then change things around and hear that person forgiving you for _____. Still look into their eyes and hear them say "I forgive you too. I really do forgive you".

## Completing the Circle

This Forgiveness Meditation starts by forgiving yourself, forgiving another person, and then, you hear them forgive you too. This is a complete circle.

This practice will eventually make things change in your mind so there will not be any guilt, frustration, sadness, anger, or making excuses for making mistakes and then feeling hard about yourself. Making excuses about anything means that one doesn't take responsibility for their own actions and this is a subtle attachment to be forgiven and let go of also.

There will develop a loving-acceptance and a true feeling of love toward that person who caused so much pain. The pain will diminish until there is only a memory of that person without any experience of grief.

Now, this is the sitting meditation, but, there is still more to the meditation and that is to forgive everything and everybody, all of the time.

## Expanding Forgiveness into Your Life

You can use forgiveness as your only object of meditation along with smiling. Forgive yourself for bumping into something or, if cooking, for cutting yourself or burning yourself or making mistakes.

Put forgiveness into everything all of the time!

Forgive thoughts for distracting you. Forgive others for distracting you. In short forgive everything all of the time. When walking from one place to another, forgive yourself and/or others. Any tiny distraction, forgive it. Forgive yourself for not remembering. Forgive yourself for making mistakes. Forgive every thought, every memory. Forgive every pain that arises. 6R and forgive ALL OF THE TIME!!! If you forget to forgive something, then forgive yourself for forgetting! Then, start again.

Do you see what I mean? It may take some time before mind begins to let go of this attachment, but, patience leads to *Nibbāna* (eventually)!

I have helped people in this type of situation and for some of them it has taken as long as one year of doing nothing else but the Forgiveness Meditation before they finally let go of the suffering and pain. This doesn't mean that they still didn't have the memories of what happened. They did. But they could reflect and remember without having any pain or suffering arise anymore. Therein lies the true healing!

So please, if you want to do this type of meditation for yourself, it would be best to get in touch with me, and stay in touch at least for a little while so I can help you to stay on the path and get it firmly going.

Grief is very strange stuff because it will come up for periods of time, even six months or a year after the event took place, and strong sadness, frustration, anger etc can arise for no apparent reason. This is why it is necessary to keep this practice going for quite some time so the attachments will eventually let go.

# 4
# Walking Meditation

To accompany Breath, Loving-kindness,
or Forgiveness practices.

## Walking Meditation Instructions

First of all, when you practice the TWIM approach to meditation, Walking Meditation is specifically used for exercise and it is to be done in between your sitting meditation sessions to keep your blood flowing so you have good energy for your investigation.

The first thing is that it's very important to remember:

SMILE all the time while you walk!
Stay with your object of meditation the entire time!
Do not put your attention on your feet!
Remember you are doing this for exercise
and walk at a normal pace.
Don't look around; keep your eyes in front of you.

Stay with your object of meditation the entire time you are walking. Keep your eyes down to the ground about 6 feet in front of you while you walk. Do not look around you with any particular interest or take a nature hike and forget your meditation.

Now, one thing that happens during retreats, and it's very frustrating to me, but I can't get people to stop doing it, is that you'll be sitting on the floor and you'll say to yourself, "Well, I'm uncomfortable." It may have been 45 minutes or an hour or something like that and then, you suddenly get up off the floor, and sit in a chair.

If you get up from the floor and just go to a chair and sit, what happens is that your mind starts to dull out because you haven't got your circulation going so well. So, don't do that! Instead, please get up and begin walking.

The Walking Meditation is every bit as important as your sitting meditation. You don't have to do the Walking Meditation super slowly, you can walk at a normal pace. Just remember to stay with your object of meditation AND relaxing all the time. Consider this as practice for continuing the meditation as you move around in your daily life.

Now, at first the Walking Meditation is going to be somewhat difficult because you're not used to it. In life you are used to walking around or going from here over to there. You're used to thinking this and thinking that and ho-humming around.

This Walking Meditation is a very important aspect to training that helps to break old habits of thinking instead of radiating Loving-kindness while you're moving in life. With this kind of walking you want to keep your meditation going on your spiritual friend from the time of your sitting, as you are getting up, and going outside to walk or, if you are using another object of meditation, you want to keep this going.

Walk no less than 15 minutes after 30 minutes of sitting meditation. When your walking is good, walk longer. You can walk up to 45 minutes. That is the maximum time. I don't think any longer than that is really useful because you get tired after that.

After you do your walking with your spiritual friend or on the breath, as the case may be, come in, sit down again and continue to do more sitting meditation.

Please understand that it is best that you sit no less, and this is sitting, not just sitting and walking—just sitting—no less than 6 hours a day during retreat times. Sit for no less than 30 minutes each time you sit and sit longer if you have a good sitting.

# Glossary of Study Terminology

## Appearing in the order of training

This glossary offers assistance with a working terminology for the TWIM practices.

This chapter has been put in the back of the book to assist the beginner and for solving any mix-up in understanding for the experienced practitioner. The definitions for terminology used in this book for training appear more or less in the order that you will have to deal with them as you learn the practice of meditation.

Buddhist Meditation shows us how mind's movements actually work. It reveals the true nature of things by uncovering the impersonal moment-to-moment process of Dependent Origination and the Four Noble Truths. The Buddha-Dhamma specifically shows us where we get caught by suffering, how this manifests first, the exact cause of it and the way out.

This journey can sometimes be difficult but it also can be magical and fun as the changes become apparent in your life and people begin to notice the change for the good in you.

As we study this, we need to understand clearly some working definitions of certain training terminology. From the beginning one learns to do this practice ALL THE TIME. So the precise definitions of terminology are very important if we are going to use this practice as our key to opening this doorway to Peace. Some of these definitions may be slightly different from what you have heard in other places. As you read further in this book, make sure the author and you are on the same page with key words, because this training is pretty important.

**Meditation** (*bhāvanā*) – observing the movements of mind's attention moment-to-moment, object-to-object for the purpose of seeing clearly the impersonal process of Dependent Origination and the Four Noble Truths.

**Mindfulness** (*Sati*) – 'Remembering' to observe the movements of mind's attention all the time.

**Awareness** (*sampajañña*) – Understanding what mind is doing; meaning whether its releasing what is arising, or getting involved with it? Is it Recognizing the movements of mind's attention, or is it moving into craving and clinging? Is it Releasing, Relaxing, Re-smiling and then Returning to the object of meditation to continue mindfulness?

**Object of Meditation** – Any object of meditation we choose is to become the home-base for re-centering during our meditation. The information we seek will not be found in the object of meditation we observe but rather it is our recognition of the impersonal Process of Dependent Origination that leads to our knowledge and vision. This occurs around the object of meditation.

**Hindrances** (*nīvarana*) – unwholesome tendencies that begin with an arising feeling that is the same as any other feeling and therefore, it should be treated in the same way during the meditation by Releasing them and not placing mind's attention on them in any way. By denying them mind's attention they will become weak and fade away.

***Jhāna*** – The definition here for '*Jhāna*' in Buddhist terms is a "stage of meditation through understanding" (the interconnectedness of the 'Four Noble Truths and Dependent Origination') and seeing how mind actually works". A *Jhāna* is a level of understanding; stage of the meditation path.

**Craving** (*taṇhā*) – the weak link in the process of Dependent Origination which manifests as tension and tightness in mind and body as it is first appearing.

The common definition for the word "Craving" is 'to want or desire', but there is much more to this word. According to the Buddha there is a definite pattern with everything that arises.

For instance, in order "to see" there is a set way things happen. First, there must be a functioning sense door such as the eye. Next there must be color and form. When the eye hits color and form then eye-consciousness arises. The meeting of these three things is called eye-contact. With eye-contact as condition eye-feeling arises. (Feeling [Vedanā] is pleasant, painful or neither painful nor pleasant and this is either physical or mental feeling.) With eye feeling as condition, then eye-craving arises.

Now 'Craving' (*taṇhā*), in all of its many different forms of seeing, hearing, tasting, smelling, bodily sensations, and thoughts, always arises as being a tension and tightness in both mind and body. 'Craving' (*taṇhā*) always manifests as the "I like it or I don't like it" mind and can be recognized as tension or tightness in both one's mind and body. This is where we come to understand the importance of the Buddha's instructions about consciously tranquilizing one's mind and body.

When the meditator has any kind of distraction arising, that pulls their attention away from their object of meditation, then a feeling immediately arises, and next, right after that the "I like it.... I don't like it" [craving-*taṇhā*] mind arising. This is sometimes seen as a big gross tightness and sometimes as a very subtle tightness or tension in mind and body.

As 'Craving' (*taṇhā*) is the cause of suffering (the Second Noble Truth) what the meditator must do is softly let go of that tension or tightness (i.e. relax) and this must consciously be done. It doesn't happen automatically as is demonstrated in the meditation instruction given to us by the Buddha. We then gently redirect mind's attention back to the object of meditation (this step is the Third Noble Truth or the cessation of craving or suffering). In practical terms this relaxing is the most important and major step that the Buddha discovered, revealing clearly the Fourth Noble Truth- that is 'the way' leading to the Cessation of Suffering.

The Buddha saw that when 'Craving' (*taṇhā*) was let go of; mind became clear, open, and very observant. He saw that the thinking mind did not arise. The thinking mind in Buddhism is called 'Clinging' (*Upādāna*).

So, when a teacher says something like "Cling to Nothing" they are actually saying to 'stop thinking about things and just observe'. This is good advice as far as it goes. Actually it would be better to say "Crave Nothing" but that would be misunderstood because the question would arise of 'how are we supposed to do that?'

"Crave Nothing" means 'to notice and let go of the tightness or tension in one's mind and body before it arises'.

How does one do this? When one sees a 'Feeling' arise, if they relax at that very moment, then the 'Craving' (*taṇhā*) won't arise. 'Craving' (*taṇhā*) is the weak link in the cycle or process of

Dependent Origination. It CAN be recognized and let go of, and when it is released then the 'Clinging' (*Upādāna*) won't arise.

One thing that has become popular today is the putting together of these two words, 'Craving/Clinging' and I think it helps to cause even more confusion. Craving' is the "I like it ... I don't like it" mind and 'Clinging' is all of the thoughts, ideas, opinions, and concepts why mind likes or dislikes a feeling when it arises. These are two very different and separate parts to the process of how things work. Putting them together just makes one's understanding of this process, even cloudier.

Some teachers today define 'Craving and Clinging' as 'Grasping'. And as I just explained that moves away from the more precise definitions that the Buddha showed us within his teaching. To eliminate clinging is not to eliminate suffering if craving is the root cause.

**No-self** (*anattā*) – Impersonal Nature; Impersonal perspective. An absence of taking anything personally which occurs during life. Seeing things purely as they are.
To do this in life, you don't have to stop using the pronouns in your language! And you don't have to try to disappear. Promise!

**Delusion** (*moha*) – In some Buddhist traditions the word "delusion" (*Moha*) is linked up with two other words which are 'Lust' (lobha) and 'Hatred' (dosa). Together these three words are sometimes called "the three poisons" and this actually is a reasonable way to look at them.

But there can be some confusion about what "delusion" (*Moha*) actually means. The Buddha meant something a little bit different every time he used this word.

According to the suttas the word 'delusion' (*Moha*) most often means 'to see whatever arises as being a personal self' (*atta*). Or we can say that 'Delusion' (*Moha*) is seeing things through the false (deluded) idea of a self (*atta*). In other words, one takes all feelings or sensations to be a part of the "I", "Me", "My", "Mine" (*atta*) identification. In Buddhism, that is delusion.

**Serenity** (*samatha*) – Here again is another word to look at. In Pāli the word is '*Samatha*'. The meaning of '*Samatha*' is tranquility, serenity, peacefulness, or stillness.

Often the common popular definition is a strongly one-pointed type of concentration, absorption concentration, or ecstatic concentration. This specific definition of serenity or tranquility certainly implies a different type of "collectedness" than the deeper types of absorption or ecstatic 'concentration'.

The goal of absorption or ecstatic concentration is to have mind stay on only one thing as if it were glued to it (to the exclusion of anything else), By comparison, '*Samatha* Collectedness' implies to have a mind that is still, serene, and calm, but alert to whatever the shifting or moving mind does moment-to-moment. Of course *Samatha/Vipassanā* (which is the standard way it is described in the suttas (see MN 149:10 where they are always linked together) leads to the total liberation of mind by seeing and recognizing how the Four Noble Truths interact with Dependent Origination. The Bodhisatta experienced firsthand, *Samatha/Vipassanā* leads directly to the end-result of *Nibbāna* and absorption or ecstatic concentration does not.

**Insight** (*Vipassanā*) – This word has a surface meaning which is 'seeing things as they truly are'.

According to the Buddha's the definition goes much deeper than that. It means 'Insight' or understanding. But understanding into what? Realizing the impersonal nature and deep understanding of the Four Noble Truths and 'HOW' Dependent Origination actually occurs with everything that arises and passes away (*anicca*) in one's mind and body. This is Buddhist Insight. In other words, one gains a deeper and deeper understanding (in each stage of *Jhāna*) of the impersonal process of 'HOW' mind and body arises through truly seeing and understanding (knowledge and vision) of the Four Noble Truths interconnection with the ongoing process of Dependent Origination.

When one can see clearly this process in all of existence, they will experience an unshakable knowledge that this is the right path to follow. Mind begins to see clearly that whatever arises and passes away (*anicca*) and that this is a part of a definite process leading us to a deep understanding that everything going on is a part of an impersonal pattern (*anattā*).

These 'Insights' can occur at any time whether one is sitting in meditation or doing their daily activities. They are quite profound when they occur.
'Insights' are like finding a lost part to a puzzle and this is where the true "aha!" experiences happen.

**Wisdom** (*paññā*) – there are many phrases within the suttas using the word 'wisdom' and they usually turn out to be concerning in some context 'the impersonal process of Dependent Origination'.

Anytime the words 'Wise Attention' or 'Wisdom' is seen in the suttas they are referring to the understanding of the Four Noble Truths and the process of Dependent Origination. Other such phrases appear as: "He sees with Wisdom", "Seeing with Wisdom", "… and his taints were destroyed by his seeing with

Wisdom...", "Wisdom", or "He is Wise".

If we can remember such instances are referring to understanding the Four Noble Truths and the process of D.O. as we read the various suttas, then our minds will open up to a new understanding of how this process and the Four Noble Truths are at the core of the teaching of the Buddha.

**Concentration** (*samādhi*) – The Pāli word actually means the unification or bringing together of mind. The word 'Collectedness' appears to be more functional for success in the meditation rather than the word 'Concentration'. In the West people take the word 'Concentration' to mean a kind of deep one-pointedness of mind or an absorbed mind and this is not what the Buddha was trying to get across. Before the time of the Buddha there were many words that described deep absorption or one-pointedness of mind. But the Buddha made up a new word. "*Samādhi*". *Samādhi* describe a completely different way of seeing and experiencing *Jhāna*. After the Buddha's *Parinibbāna*, because this word was very popular, the Brahmins of that time changed the definition of '*samādhi*' back to mean—'strong one-pointedness'. But, the Buddha was showing that there is a difference between a 'Collected Mind' and a strongly absorbed or 'Concentrated Mind'.

The words 'Collected Mind" (*Samādhi*) give us the idea of a mind that is composed, calm, still, and very alert. This kind of mind observes whenever mind's attention shifts from one thing to another. A 'Concentrated' mind, on the other hand, means that mind is stuck on one thing to the exclusion of anything else that may try to arise. So a 'Concentrated' Mind' by this definition loses full awareness and mindfulness (*Sati*) of what is happening in the present moment because it is only seeing the one thing it is pointing at. This statement also refers to "access or neighborhood concentration" (*upacāra samādhi*) and "moment-to-moment concentration" (*khanika samādhi*). Why?

The simple answer is there is no tranquilizing of mind and body before the meditator brings their attention back to the object of meditation. Because of this, there is no lowering of tension in mind or body or seeing of how the Four Noble Truths and Dependent Origination actually work. One does not realize how craving (tightness and tension) is brought back to the meditation object.

This is why when the teachers of straight *'Vipassanā'* tell their students that 'Absorption Concentration' won't ever lead to *Nibbāna*, they are 100% correct. Any kind of practice which divides *'Samatha* Meditation' and *'Vipassanā* Meditation' into two different practices, can't possibly lead one to *Nibbāna*. Why?

Because mind has the need to be calm, composed, and clear, while it is in a *Jhāna*, in order to see clearly the interconnectedness of the Four Noble Truths and Dependent Origination. This is why the practice of straight *Vipassanā* has some serious students. The Buddha taught us to practice *'Samatha/Vipassanā'* together and this is the difference between commentary based meditation practice and the sutta approach to meditation.

The results of these two practices are different. One-pointed 'Concentration' is not the same kind of mental development that the Buddha shows us. The Buddha taught us to tranquilize our mind and body every time mind's attention shifts from one thing to another. The 'Collected Mind" is not so deeply one-pointed that the force of one's 'Concentration' causes mind to stay on one object of meditation, even if that attention 'Concentrates' on something momentarily.

The 'Collected Mind' is able to observe how mind's attention goes from one thing to another, very precisely. There is much more full awareness of both mind and body here than with a deeply 'Concentrated' one-pointed mind or absorbed mind'. This is why I choose to use the word 'Collected' rather than 'Concentrated" mind. By using the word "Collected" there is less confusion about the kind of meditation that the Buddha is referring to and it is easier to understand the descriptions given in the suttas.

The words listed here are a good start for you with which to work on this approach to the meditation.

# About the Author

 Most Venerable Bhante Vimalaraṁsi Mahāthera became a Buddhist monk in 1986 because of his keen interest in meditation. He went to Burma in 1988 to practice intensive meditation at the famous meditation center, Mahasi Yeiktha in Rangoon. While there, he practiced meditation for 20 to 22 hours a day for three months and 16 hours a day for 5 months. Because of some social unrest, all foreigners were asked to leave the country. So Bhante traveled to Malaysia and practiced intensive Loving-kindness Meditation for 6 months.

In 1990, Bhante went back to Burma for more intensive *Vipassanā* meditation, for 14 to 16 hours a day, at Chanmyay Yeiktha in Rangoon. He practiced for 2 years, sometimes sitting in meditation for as long as 7 to 8 hours a sitting. After two years of intensive meditation and experiencing what they said was the final result, he became very disillusioned with the straight *Vipassanā* method and left Burma to continue his search.

He went back to Malaysia and began teaching Loving-kindness Meditation. In 1995, Bhante was invited to live and teach at the largest Theravāda monastery in Malaysia. This Sri Lankan monastery offered public talks every Friday evening and Sunday morning where 300 to 500 people would attend. Bhante gave talks every other Friday and on every Sunday.

While staying there he had the opportunity to meet many learned monks, and Bhante questioned them at length about the Buddha's Teachings. He found out that the straight *Vipassanā* Burmese method of meditation is taken from a commentary written a thousand years after the Buddha's death, called the Visuddhi Magga. This commentary is not very accurate when compared directly with the sutta teachings. Bhante Vimalaraṁsi then began to study the sutta texts more thoroughly and practice meditation according to these texts. After a three month self-retreat, he came back to Malaysia and wrote a book on the Mindfulness of Breathing called "The Ānāpānasati Sutta – A Practical Guide to Mindfulness of Breathing and Tranquil Wisdom Meditation". There are now over 1,000,000 copies distributed worldwide in multiple languages. This book is currently used as a practical study guide for meditation teachers and their students.

Bhante Vimalaraṁsi came back to the U.S. in 1998 and has been teaching meditation throughout the country since then. In 2003 he cofounded the United International Buddha-Dhamma Society. UIBDS supports the Dhamma Sukha Meditation Center located near Annapolis, Missouri, USA, where he teaches meditation from May–October each year.

In 2008 he officially announced the birth of the Buddhist American Forest Tradition in Annapolis, MO. This is the first Buddhist American Forest Tradition study center on American soil where all teaching and work is done using English as the primary language and the core teachings rely on the Pāli Canon directly with the Vissudhi Magga used as an additional reference support. The Tradition actually began in 2005.

International monks now come there to improve their English and study more deeply the meditation and sutta studies. An active ordination program is available where both men and women are trained equally.

# About Dhamma Sukha Meditation Center

United International Buddha-Dhamma Society (UIBDS) and Dhamma Sukha Meditation Center (DSMC) are located on 103 acres of forested land located in the Ozark Mountains of Iron County (near to Annapolis) in Missouri, USA.

DSMC's goal is to be open all year round. At present it usually houses from 10–20 students at a time between the months of May 15–October 15 each year for meditation training and Buddhist studies. In winter it is open for visitors and there are small group retreats. The main teachers usually teach abroad during the coldest time of the year. This helps to raise money for further buildings at the center. Presently there are cabins, dining hall and kitchen, library, and a new Dhamma hall is going up in 2012. There are beautiful walking trails and flat areas for walking near the main halls. There is a lay area for meditators and a separate monastics living area.

June–October full moons serve as the center's Rains Retreat period each year. Monastics may come in for a May to September Rains Retreat if they let us know in advance. We do offer an Dhamma English support program.

In this Buddhist tradition, Rains Retreat is when monks and

nuns stay in one place to give Dhamma talks and teach people meditation. They also practice their own meditation deeply at this time. Each year various monastics who also support the goals of this program visit from different traditions. Often times they will offer to teach Buddhist history, Chanting, and Pāli classes while in the center. From over 23 countries around the world, students and faithful lay people come to investigate early Buddhist teachings and they stay from 2 weeks to 3 months at a time upon by approval by the teacher.

There is also an active ordination program for men and women for equal training. It is a sincere forest training which is received and there will be opportunities in the near future for study abroad at a university in Sri Lanka which is now partnering with the DSMC project in 2012.

DSMC is dedicated a religious center sheltered by United International Buddha-Dhamma Society. UIBDS is a Missouri 501 (c) (3) non-profit corporation set up for the purpose of Religious, Charitable and Educational works.

DSMC provides a support place for people to come and hear early Buddhist texts taught in English by a master meditation teacher, Most Venerable Bhante Vimalaraṁsi Mahāthera and Sasana Dipika Sister Khema who have both taught this Buddha-Dhamma internationally over recent past years.

In the center you will study and practice early foundation teachings recovered from the very earliest Buddhist texts that survived. Center monastics offer free counseling support for people. Daily meditation is practiced and many supports are in place to help students keep their practice going in life.

After 14 years of investigation work, at DSMC, it has been

confirmed that the Buddha recovered something extremely unique that leads directly to a reduction of suffering and, if the teachings and meditation are pursued more deeply, following the precise instructions, this training can lead to an eventual total cessation of suffering in this lifetime.

The center teaches a simple meditation practice based on Right Effort as found in the early texts. The practice is called Tranquil Wisdom Insight Meditation, TWIM for short. TWIM is easy and fun to learn and is appropriate for anyone within the bounds of any religion.

This teaching is easy to understand and immediately effective. The practice transfers very well into daily life to help us lighten up, smile more, and become happier. It is so progressively interesting that it invites deeper inspection and people really do want to 'come and see' and understand more.

 There is no question that Buddhist teachings make life easier. They provide a clear understanding of how the mind works. As you discover how things actually operate, then quite naturally, as you calm down, you will tend to act in more compassionate ways towards people in daily life.

Training at the center uses the Majjhima Nikāya as a main text for guidance during your training. Students who practice in earnest and want to progress well are encouraged to follow the advice of MN-95 The Canki Sutta when coming to the center to study. In that sutta there are 12 steps key to making good progress. MN-15 describes the best student for the teacher to put time and energy into training. The proper outcome of your training is described in MN-21. It is worth it for you to investigate these suttas before coming to train.

At the center, students and monastics alike are challenged to test their understanding through their own investigation for verification of any spoken truth they hear in a Dhamma talk. If their results match the results described within the suttas, then they are considered the Buddha's teaching. If not, then its time for open Dhamma discussion and re-evaluation.

**More Information**

We encourage you to visit our website at www.dhammasukha. org

At the website you will find a lot more information about Dhamma talks, how we teach at the center, books that can help you, articles, and more information about how to contact our center in Missouri.

If you need help, you can write to Rev. Sister Khema at sisterkhema@yahoo.com. She will forward you to whomever can help you best.

Please make arrangements to come into the center by April 15 if possible so residences can be carefully planned for you.

The address of Dhamma Sukha Meditation Center and Anathapindika's Park is:

**Dhamma Sukha Meditation Center**
**8218 County Road 204**
**Annapolis, MO 63620 USA**

Website: www.dhammasukha.org
Office Telephone: (573) 546-1214 (please leave a clear message)
E-mail: bhantev4u@dhammasukha.org,
Training Questions: sisterkhema@dhammasukha.org
Administrator and Registration: davidjohnson@yahoo.com

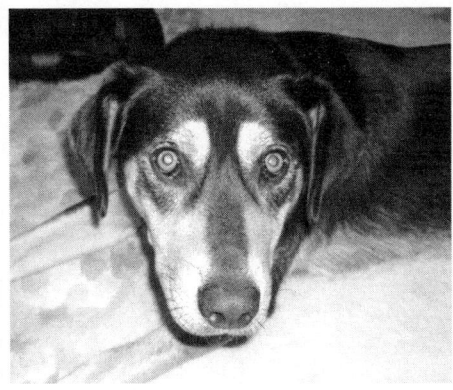

Rex, 2008–present:
protector of the center.

Rex and Buddy, 2009:
Breath of Love—Friends Forever!

Grandmother Silky:
who keeps everyone in line.

Smiley, 2004-2008:
babysitter for the students.